Breastfeeding Grief

Understanding and Recovery

Lucy Ruddle, IBCLC

Praeclarus Press. LLC
©2024 Lucy Ruddle. All rights reserved
www.PraeclarusPress.com

Praeclarus Press, LLC
2504 Sweetgum Lane
Amarillo, Texas 79124 USA
806-367-9950
www.PraeclarusPress.com

DISCLAIMER

The information contained in this publication is advisory only and is not intended to replace sound clinical judgment or individualized patient care. The author disclaims all warranties, whether expressed or implied, including any warranty as the quality, accuracy, safety, or suitability of this information for any particular purpose.

ISBN: 978-1-946665-75-1

Cover Design: Ken Tackett
Copyediting: Chris Tackett
Layout & Design: Nelly Murariu
Copyright © 2024 Lucy Ruddle

A note on language

You will see throughout this book that I use a range of words to describe breastfeeding, chestfeeding, mums, and parents. It is important to me that my work speaks to as many people as possible, and while the majority of people this book is aimed at will use mother/ mom/mum, and she/her pronouns, some won't, and those people are at increased risk of not feeling supported or heard in their experiences. In addition, for some, the word breast can trigger a trauma response due to a history of sexual or physical abuse. Where studies refer only to mothers, so do I. Where I know a parent's pronouns, I use them accordingly. By using a wide range of language, it is my hope that everyone feels represented and no one feels erased.

Contents

Introduction

When I was expecting my first baby, I knew I was going to breast-feed him. I remember a conversation with a friend, who advised me to buy a particular brand of formula, and I was irritated that she'd even suggest it to me. "But I'm going to breastfeed," I re-sponded, face screwed up with annoyance. My friend smiled and didn't say anything else. Several weeks later, I found myself sitting on the kitchen floor, sobbing uncontrollably because my newborn wanted to feed *again*, and my nipples were so cracked and blis-tered that I couldn't face yet another feeding session. Soon after, I decided to stop breastfeeding and I still remember how the agony of my engorged breasts felt like a deserved punishment for not "trying hard enough" and gritting my teeth through the pain that was every feed.

Perhaps you were like me. When you were expecting your baby, you might have imagined breastfeeding as a peaceful and beautiful experience that simply worked. Equally, you may not have considered breastfeeding much at all, except to figure that you'd give it a go, but you'd just use formula if it didn't work. Maybe you had seen other people struggle with breastfeeding, but you were determined that you wouldn't fail, and you spent your pregnancy reading lactation books, watching YouTube videos, and following breastfeeding specialists on social media.

However you felt about breastfeeding before your baby is born, it's likely that once your little one entered the world, breastfeeding became more important to you than ever before. This sudden, new importance may be at least partly linked to the hormonal changes that occur when you give birth. When you subsequently ran into challenges with feeding your baby, it's likely that, sooner or later, you began to feel that you were failing your baby. Perhaps you stopped breastfeeding altogether like I did, or combination fed with a sense of guilt or shame.

Some of the difficult feelings many parents hold around the end of their breastfeeding journey are partly due to more hormonal shifts as lactation stops, and partly down to living in a world that doesn't know how to offer gentle, loving support without opinion or advice. Perhaps most significantly, it can be a result of society having simply forgotten how to make breastfeeding work, meaning that the support families need to breastfeed is just not there anymore.

My goal with this book is to help you to feel better about your infant feeding journey, and I base my approach primarily on lived experience supporting real families rather than academia. However, this book is evidence-based to back up my experiences, and citations are listed throughout and in the back, if you do want to dig more deeply into the topics discussed.

Part one of this book explores many of the reasons for breastfeeding failure and associated grief or distress. Part two has practical exercises and techniques for you to work through as and when you would like.

By the end of this book, you will not only have an understanding of why and how you experienced breastfeeding in the way you did, but you will also have several tools to help you move through the grieving process and recover. We know that if you are unable to process your feelings safely, you are likely to feel worse for longer. This sort of incomplete grief often leads to fear, anger, depression, anxiety, and isolation. I want you to be able to move through your feelings and come out the other side feeling hopeful, and proud of what you achieved.

How Many of These Boxes Can You Tick?

☐ I didn't get the information I needed during pregnancy.

☐ My baby was removed from me during the first hour after birth (even if just for weighing).

☐ Someone latched my baby for their first breastfeed instead of waiting for my baby to latch independently.

☐ I had pain that was dismissed, downplayed, or I wasn't properly supported in how to resolve it.

☐ My family were well-meaning but not up to date on breastfeeding information.

☐ Someone in my family didn't really want me to breastfeed.

☐ When I ran into problems, formula was suggested, even though I didn't want to use it.

☐ I was advised to stop breastfeeding by a medical professional.

☐ I was told Fed is Best and/or Breast is Best.

☐ It was hard to find truly well qualified breastfeeding support that was accessible to me.

☐ I wasn't told about options such as seeing an IBCLC.

The above statements represent common experiences of many mothers and birthing parents. They all undermine breastfeeding, and none of these experiences are your fault. We will explore more about this later, but for now, I hope you can take comfort in knowing that you are not alone, and you are *not* to blame.

PART ONE:
UNDERSTANDING

CHAPTER ONE

What You Might be Feeling

If you picked up this book, it is likely that you are dealing with some uncomfortable or unexpected feelings about your experience of lactation and infant feeding. You might be wondering if these feelings are normal, or even "okay," and you might be surprised by their intensity. Equally, you might be worried that you're not feeling "enough" about your breastfeeding journey, perhaps questioning whether you are numb to it, or blocking your experience out, anticipating those feelings might pop up unwanted if you have another baby.

In this chapter, we will focus on the very real feelings many mothers experience regarding breastfeeding either ending early or not going the way that they had hoped and planned for. Primarily, we will be talking about these feelings as grief. However, it's important to acknowledge that not everyone experiences a sense of grief, and that is also okay. Take what resonates, leave what doesn't.

Grief

We tend to think of grief as something we experience when a loved one dies. However, grief is defined in *Merriam-Webster* as, "A deep and poignant distress caused by **or as if by** bereavement" and "A cause of such suffering."

Essentially, grief can be described as an expression of loss. We may feel grief when a friend moves away, when a pet goes missing, during divorce, or if we lose a much-loved job. We can also feel grief when breastfeeding ends before we want it to, especially if that ending is surrounded with difficult experiences such as pain, worries about your baby's health, or your abilities as a parent. You have lost something important to you–a relationship and a way of parenting that you worked hard at. Despite this hard work, lactation still ended. That is a big deal–grief is understandable and valid.

Grief is an entirely normal process to go through. However, it's often hugely mismanaged in the Western world. There are often conflicting feelings that are confusing. Maybe you feel deep sadness at the end of your breastfeeding experience, but you might also feel relief that the battle is over. When it comes to breastfeeding, in particular, the people around you might be focused on what they see as the positives to try and cheer you up. However, as anyone who has experienced grief will tell you, trying to cheer someone up can lead to them feeling dismissed, belittled, and even angry. Feelings of confusion and frustration can then come up, leading you to isolate yourself. You might simply stop talking about your feelings, or you might actively avoid other people. I have spoken to many mums who say that they couldn't go to baby groups anymore after they stopped breastfeeding – it was too upsetting for them to see other parents breastfeeding. Burying your feelings in this way will not help you to process them and recover from your grief around your breastfeeding relationship.

There are several stages of grief, which you may have heard about before. These are:

- Denial
- Anger
- Bargaining
- Depression
- Acceptance

While the stages of grief are helpful for a basic understanding of your experience, it's important to know that our feelings are more complex than a checklist. You can move in and out of these stages at any time, they are often not felt in order, and some stages may be skipped over altogether. For example, we frequently don't see denial regarding grieving lactation, but we do tend to see a lot of anger and depression.

It might be more helpful to focus on the common reactions discussed in a fantastic book *The Grief Recovery Handbook* by John James and Russell Friedman. These reactions are:

- Reduced concentration/forgetfulness
- Numbness
- Disrupted sleep patterns (sleeping less or more than usual)
- Changed eating habits (eating more or less than is normal for you)
- A rollercoaster of feelings leading to feeling exhausted

These reactions are normal and commonly experienced in all types of grief. Notice that they are not stages; they are simply feelings and experiences through which you will move in different ways, at different times, and at different intensities.

Please be reassured that grief can be recovered from. In fact, you experience grief recovery any time you get over a relationship breakup, pet loss, job loss, house move, the end of a friendship, etc. If you take nothing else from this chapter, remember that you won't always feel this way.

A good starting point for recovery is to talk about your feelings, but there are many more things you can do as and when you feel able. The second part of this book is dedicated to that.

The rest of this chapter looks at a whole range of feelings you might be dealing with. You might not personally be dealing with a grieving process as your breastfeeding journey ends or unfolds in a way that you didn't want, but you may very well find similarities between your feelings now and the feelings you have had at times of grief.

Shame

Even the word "shame" can feel uncomfortable! It's one of the feelings we tend to avoid talking about, and you may even work hard to actively avoid feeling this emotion. In fact, the need to silence shame can be so intense for some people that it might culminate in addictions being born because of that desperation (Milan & Varescon, 2022; Matthews, 2019).

Shame is a complex and incredibly uncomfortable emotion that can arise from a range of situations. It often stems from our fear of judgment and rejection from others, as well as the pressure we tend to feel to maintain a certain image of ourselves. The fear of looking vulnerable or flawed can intensify our experience of shame. However, it's important to recognize that shame is a universal emotion that people experience at different points across their lives. It's also worth noting that vulnerability can actually foster deeper connections and understanding with others, rather than leading to the rejection we fear. While it can be difficult to open up about our shame triggers, sharing our experiences with trusted individuals or seeking support can help to reduce feelings of isolation. It can also give us opportunities for learning, growth, and self-compassion. Remember that no one is perfect, and embracing our vulnerabilities can lead to personal growth and stronger connections with others. It's important to create a safe space for ourselves where we can acknowledge and talk about our shame, allowing for healing and self-acceptance to occur.

Shame is a feeling that many parents express to me when we talk about their breastfeeding journey ending, and it's often formed on a foundation of feeling like they have failed. If you're unable to breastfeed, the next logical step a lot of parents take is "I've failed as a parent." If you have failed as a parent, then shame is right there to take you deep into its pit of despair and self-loathing. If you're someone who also happens to work in some capacity with lactation, this feeling of shame can be even bigger because you're trained in breastfeeding. You may wonder how you can support other people to breastfeed if you couldn't do it yourself.

So, shame is a fear of being perceived as bad, lacking, neglectful, lazy, or any other number of words we often see thrown around. When you have been told all through pregnancy that breastfeeding is really important, when you've confidently told your friends and family that you *will* be breastfeeding, and you then need to stop or take a different path, it is entirely logical that you might feel some degree of shame. You have to admit to yourself and to the people around you that you couldn't do something that has been labelled as incredibly important.

Do you want to know a secret about shame, though? It's like the monster under the bed, in that it quickly shrinks away when you shine a light on it. Brene Brown's work on shame is at this point almost universally known and respected. She has found through her research that the light we need to shine on shame is talking about it. Once we are brave enough to disclose our feelings and to see that the people around us do not actually recoil in horror, shame shrinks and eventually disappears altogether. Community, active listening, and love are all tools that help to overcome shame.

Guilt

Guilt can feel similar to shame, but it's a little different. Guilt is something that often comes up when we've done something that goes against our conscience or belief system, whereas shame is fuelled by the fear of other people's reactions or feelings towards us. So, if you feel guilty about not meeting your breastfeeding goal then it's likely that breastfeeding was important to you on a deep level. While guilt does serve some purposes (it can make us change our behaviour in a positive way), it can also make things worse for us.

There was a fascinating study carried out in 2007, where the researchers asked women to break their diets with donuts and sweets. One group were reassured about doing this to ease their guilt, while the other group were simply left in silence with their guilty thoughts and feelings. Can you guess which group ate the most food? It was the group left to feel guilty. Guilt spurred the behaviour that the participants were trying to restrict. In fact, the guilty group ate about 70g of sweets, compared to the other group, who ate around 28g on average (Adams & Leary, 2007). This is helpful for us when dealing with the topic of guilt around breastfeeding because it shows that your guilt, while a common feeling, isn't actually serving you. It also shows that, like shame, talking about it helps. Of course, understanding that and relieving it are two different things. If it was easy to stop feeling guilty, breastfeeding grief would be a lot simpler to overcome. However, my hope is that once you read this book, you will see that your guilt is misplaced; you fought a hard fight, you didn't simply abandon your beliefs about the value of human milk.

Anger

When it comes to breastfeeding, the expectations placed on new parents can be overwhelming. Society expects us to breastfeed, and for some, the inability to meet these expectations can lead to feelings of anger. Anger here is a well-placed emotion, and it's essential you feel that you can acknowledge and express it. Hormonal changes during pregnancy, the postnatal period, and as you adjust to stopping breastfeeding can also contribute to these emotions, applying even more pressure. While we have made great strides in gender equality, the patriarchal society we live in still very much influences the lack of support for new mothers. You will often find yourself left alone with your anger, not knowing if it's safe or acceptable to express it. It's not very "ladylike" to scream and rage, is it?

Anger is often present when someone is processing a difficult breastfeeding experience, but because of how society treats anger (especially in women and female-presenting individuals), we tend to mask it. You may not feel any anger right now (unless, perhaps, it's directed at yourself), but if you stay with me through this book, it's likely to bubble up as you realise how much society is failing us in our desire to breastfeed. Anger is a healthy emotion. I invite you to feel it fully. Anger gives us motion, energy, and the motivation to act against the injustices we have been dealt.

Depression

Depression and failure to breastfeed are closely linked in studies. Prof. Amy Brown's work in this area found that Postnatal Depression was more likely to present in women who had wanted to breastfeed but stopped before reaching their goal. This isn't a surprise to me, given that depression thrives on feelings of failure, shame, and guilt. It goes much deeper than that, though. There are several hormones and experiences associated with breastfeeding that might protect against postnatal depression, as long as breastfeeding is working well for the parent and infant. Oxytocin is a wonderful hormone that is present in high amounts every time you latch your baby to your breast. You may well have heard it referred to as the Love Hormone, thanks to its powerful ability to make us feel relaxed, content, and "loved up." Kathleen Kendall-Tackett has taken things to an even more fascinating level in her research, where she discusses how breastfeeding can reduce inflammation in the body, by reducing the levels of stress hormones floating about. Reduced inflammation and reduced stress hormones = happier, healthier mum (Kendall-Tackett, 2007)!

If you stop breastfeeding, not only do you suddenly have less oxytocin in your system, but you're also going to be dealing with your feelings of guilt, sadness, shame, anger, etc., *and* given the way our Western world treats new mothers, you are probably having those feelings dismissed or silenced. Postnatal Depression is only a small sidestep away.

Trauma

In her book, *Why Breastfeeding Grief and Trauma Matter*, Prof. Amy Brown describes how parents can feel genuine trauma when they are unable to meet their breastfeeding goals. This might sound extreme, and, in fact, some people don't like it when we use the word "trauma" to describe how women and parents can feel after breastfeeding ends. However, the International Classification of Diseases defines trauma as:

> *A delayed or protracted response to a stressful event or situation (of either brief or long duration) of an excep-tionally threatening or catastrophic nature, which is likely to cause pervasive distress in almost anyone (https:// estss.org/learn-about-trauma/icd10/).*

Anybody who has experienced putting themselves through the often extreme pain of breastfeeding a baby with a shallow latch over and over again, every 2 hours or more, for days, weeks, or months at a time would quite likely be dealing with an event that the body and brain perceive to be threatening and catastrophic, which absolutely leads to pervasive distress. I have worked with several clients over the years who have been breastfeeding through unimaginable nipple trauma, even to the point where chunks of their nipples have been missing. Despite these injuries, the mothers continued to feed. They simply bite down on a mus-lin, their hand, or the inside of their cheeks to try and distract them from the pain. In what other situation would you deliberate-ly and repeatedly put yourself through something so damaging?

Then we need to consider the psychology and biology of moth-erhood, especially in regard to infant feeding. On a basic level, after you give birth, your body expects to lactate. If that lactation is ended abruptly, the resulting crash in hormones often leads to depression. There is also a theory that ending breastfeeding suddenly mimics the experience of infant loss. On a deep level it's possible your brain views this sudden, early end to lactation as the result of a death or separation.

Now, let's remember that all through pregnancy, you are told how important breastfeeding is. When you are faced with being told or feeling like you need to give your baby formula, it can cause some intense feelings of guilt, anxiety, and fear. If every time you make your baby a bottle you are exposed to those feelings again, it's only a matter of time before you might meet the criteria for trauma.

Relief

Amongst all the murky feelings, you may also experience relief. This in itself can make some mums feel guilty and ashamed. Another view is that, of course you might feel relief. If breastfeeding was a constant battle of one kind or another, it is natural to exhale a sense of "thank goodness that's over" when you stop. You were putting yourself in a situation that was emotionally and/or physically painful multiple times every single day. You may have been worrying at every single feed ("Is the latch okay?" "Is the baby swallowing?" "How bad is the pain going to be?" "Do I have to feed in public?" "Will I experience this gender dysphoria at every feed?"). Relief is just as normal as all of the other feelings that can come up at this time.

As I mentioned earlier, relief is often present in all types of grief. If a loved one died after a long, painful illness, you would feel sadness at the loss, as well as relief that the person is no longer suffering. If you lost a job, you might be angry, confused, and sad, but you might also feel some relief that you no longer have to worry about deadlines. Relief at no longer needing to put yourself through pain and anxiety several times a day is completely valid.

CHAPTER TWO

Fed Isn't Best, but Breast Isn't Either

It's common when you tell people that you've stopped breastfeeding for them to respond with a platitude such as "Well, fed is best, after all!" or "Happy mummy, happy baby!" People tend to say things like this because they want to reassure you that you're doing the right thing, and it doesn't matter how your baby is fed. There are several reasons why hearing these platitudes may not sit well with you, though, which I'll talk more about shortly.

Equally, there are also challenges with the phrase "breast is best," which likely sets people up to feel that they've failed when breastfeeding is hard. It can make you feel that you're being pressured into breastfeeding, and it implies that if you can't do it, you're not doing the best for you or your baby.

Let's get a little deeper into the challenges surrounding statements of something being "best" in the world of infant feeding.

Dismissal of Feelings

Most importantly to me, the short, pithy statements typically used when lactation ends early are excellent at shutting down conversation and stopping the parent from talking about their feelings on the matter. Yet, we know that talking things through, acknowledging feelings, and processing them is what leads to healing. The problem is that society is not good at holding space for hard feelings, letting people express sadness or grief, or, heaven forbid, seeing someone cry. A lot of people feel uncomfortable when faced with someone else's messy feelings and will (consciously or otherwise) try to stop those feelings for their own comfort. Other people just want to help but don't know how, so offer words that they hope are reassuring but accidently shut down discussion. When it comes to infant feeding challenges, shutting down feelings commonly leads to parents feeling silenced and invalidated, and ashamed or embarrassed that they tried to admit to how they were feeling in the first place. Of course, we know that internalising our feelings to make other people more comfortable doesn't help us to shake those feelings off. It just buries them.

Discounting Your Wishes

If you wanted to improve your fitness or take an evening class, you would hope to have those desires taken seriously. You certainly wouldn't expect to be told that those things aren't important, or even hear that you're being selfish and all that matters is that your partner/child is healthy! We have come a long way over the last several decades when it comes to supporting women with achieving their goals, but somehow, when it comes to breastfeeding, we are still stuck in a narrative where the parent's very real, valid, and important wishes about how they feed their baby are completely discounted in favour of platitudes. This can send a strong message to a new parent that *they* aren't important anymore. While we absolutely need to protect the health and happiness of infants, a huge part of that protection has to do with the emotional state of the baby's parents. A parent who feels she needs to sacrifice their own wishes as long as their baby is happy is on a fast track to burnout, resentment, and postnatal depression.

Undermining Informed Choice

On a basic level, fed isn't an *option*; it is the minimum requirement, so it clearly isn't "best." A happy mummy isn't guaranteed because she's stopped breastfeeding, either. In fact, the evidence tells us that you're more likely to feel depressed if you stop breastfeeding earlier than you wanted to. How can you make an informed choice about feeding your baby when you are faced with statements like "fed is best?" Informed choice leads to empowerment and confidence, and ultimately, healing. But we often don't get that opportunity, so instead, we bury the feelings, and they come to the surface any time we see someone else breastfeeding, read about something amazing breastmilk can do, or see the warning label on a tin of formula.

An Excuse for Poor Lactation Support

When a healthcare provider tells you "Ah well, fed is best" or "You tried your best. Don't worry about it," what they could actually be saying to you is; "I don't have the skills or resources to support you to meet your breastfeeding goal." This is *not* the fault of the professional. This is usually down to a lack of funding, which, in turn, is down to lack of interest from the government. Unfortunately, this lack of time and training is contributing to a negative impact on breastfeeding rates and maternal mental health.

In addition, it's also possible that some of the healthcare professionals supporting you with infant feeding have had their own difficult experiences, which they haven't been able to process (for the same reasons as everyone else). This lack of support, lack of debriefing, and lack of training can all combine and result in them offering support, which is biased and even laced with their own trauma.

Because we do have formula, and because using it is so common, it's easy for health professionals to simply direct you to that under the guide of "fed is best" than it is to access the training and debriefing that could allow them to support you with actually meeting your lactation goal.

Advice to Breastfeed Without Appropriate Support

"Breast is Best" infuriates me. It tells you to breastfeed but does nothing to address the fact that so many people find breast-feeding hard. It feels to me like when you see those pictures of smokers' lungs on cigarette packets but without providing funding for smoking cessation support. Your national health organisation gets to say, "We're doing something about this" without spending much money or *doing* anything meaningful ("Yay! Breast is best! But you'll have to figure out how to do it on your own because we aren't going to improve access to skilled lactation support").

If you contact your Member of Parliament (MP) in the UK about breastfeeding funding, they will proudly tell you that they have provided £50 million of funding to the NHS for breastfeeding support since 2021. As a comparison, the UK government's personal expenses for politicians regularly exceeds £100 million per year, and the NHS spends around £80 million per year on prescribing paracetamol (Briefing: The cost of MPs in 2020-21). In short, £50 million is barely a drop in the ocean.

Dividing Parents into Camp Breast or Camp Bottle

There shouldn't be this divide we see between parents based on how they feed their babies. We shouldn't be in Fed is Best or Breast is Best camps, arguing with each other about who's lazy and who's bashing who. While we're busy doing this, no one is focussing on making governments work harder to help more people reach whatever feeding goal they have in mind. When we segregate parents based on their feeding method, we create an environment of "us vs. them" instead of one of understanding and support for everyone. Parenting is hard. We are *all* being let down in one way or another by this sort of separation.

Profits Over Health

Formula companies spend a lot of time and money trying to persuade the public that they exist to protect babies and look after families. However, their history of predatory marketing tells a different story. Abbott (a US formula company who provide about 40% of the formula in the States) reported a jump in profits between 2020 and 2022 from $3.6 billion to $7.1 billion (The Guardian, 2022). On the other hand, the US spent $90 million on its Peer support WIC (Women, Infants, and Children) program and a little under $10 million on hospital lactation support in 2023 (usbreastfeeding.org). The UK doesn't present a better picture. Our formula market is worth £1.4 billion (and as discussed in the above section, our government has only allocated £50 million to support breastfeeding).

The truly worrying thing in all of this though, is the number of lives that could be saved each year if breastfeeding rates increased. According to the WHO, the lives of 820,000 babies around the world could be saved every year if more was done to support breastfeeding (WHO, 2018). People tend to assume this only applies to developing countries, but a report commissioned by UNICEF revealed that an increase in breastfeeding rates in the UK would save the NHS £40 million in hospital admissions (RCPCH Position Statement, 2022).

I know that reading these statistics can be upsetting, but please remember that this isn't about you as a parent; it is not *your* fault that our breastfeeding rates are so low, or that you couldn't reach your lactation goal. This is a profits-over-health situation, where funding is not being properly allocated to new parents and their babies. These statistics can absolutely make us angry, but I invited you to direct that anger towards government and industry, not yourself.

CHAPTER THREE

What Good Breastfeeding Support Looks Like

If I'm going to convince you that you didn't fail to breastfeed but that our society failed you instead, it makes sense to talk about the support you might have access to as a standard if we lived in a world that really wanted you to meet your goals. The following sections are not just my vision for improved breastfeeding support; these areas have been discussed by other authors and researchers for some time now. For a much deeper look into this topic, I recommend Amy Brown's book *Breastfeeding Uncovered*.

In Pregnancy

Many studies have looked at whether lactation education in pregnancy is helpful for breastfeeding success after the baby is born. The short answer is yes, it is. A 2022 systematic review concluded that breastfeeding education led to more parents breastfeeding for longer and with confidence (Kehinde, O'Donnell, & Grealish, 2023).

However, it's important to understand that good lactation education needs to be more than a one-size-fits-all class. A 2020 study found that individualised education addressing the concerns unique to each family was noticeably more helpful for increasing breastfeeding success than other types of information. In this study, 70% of women were still breastfeeding at 4 months after receiving the personalised education during pregnancy, compared to 46% of mothers who had only accessed generic support (Huang, Yao, Liu, & Luo, 2019). What does personalised support mean? Well, obviously, it depends on the individual family. However, some examples include:

- Addressing concerns about milk supply after not reaching their lactation goals with their first baby.
- Teaching that cluster feeding is normal and not a sign of low milk supply to a family heavily influenced by an older family member who raised their babies on routine.
- Supporting induced lactation for a two-mum family.
- Discussing managing gender dysphoria for a trans dad.
- Preparing a survivor of sexual abuse for potential triggers around their breasts.
- Having a plan for nighttime parenting.

Currently, the breastfeeding discussion you can expect to have with your care provider in the UK during your pregnancy tends to be along the lines of "Breast is best. Here's a leaflet, and we have a free workshop, but the next one isn't until after your due date/is in the middle of the working day, so you might miss it."

If you do get along to the free class, you'll likely find yourself clutching a child's preloved doll while pointing its nose at your nipple, which is covered by your bra and top, so you're not *quite* sure if you're even doing it right. *Surely,* you may find yourself thinking, *a real baby would move around a bit more?*

You will be told a list of health benefits for you and your baby if you breastfeed, and the message will typically be that breast is best. Formula will not be mentioned at all. While the reasoning for this is sound, it can easily create a feeling of shame or othering for parents who have questions about combination feeding or what to do if breastfeeding doesn't go according to plan.

You'll also probably be shown a bunch of grapes and be informed that this is what it looks like inside your breast. While this is interesting to know, it doesn't really help you to actually breastfeed your baby. It would be more helpful to spend extra time talking about cluster feeding, for example.

While the above examples aren't harmful or wrong, many parents report finding this approach not particularly helpful. According to research by Prof. Amy Brown (2016), the women she interviewed wanted breastfeeding education in pregnancy to:

- Focus on breastfeeding being normal, not "best."
- Explore more reasons to breastfeed than just the health benefits.
- Carry a message that "Every Feed Counts," not just exclusive breastfeeding.
- Target family members and wider society, not just the mother or lactating parent.

Taking all of this into consideration, along with the evidence we have that individualised lactation education is most effective, gives us a great starting point for understanding the flaws in the current standardised approach to antenatal information and can create a foundation for improved education and, therefore, less parents feeling they've failed.

The Hours After Birth

It's still common practice to whip a freshly born baby way from their parents to weigh and administer vitamin K. However, it's now understood that the first hour after birth is a unique time, and the skin-to-skin contact between mother and baby during this sacred time should not be interrupted unless absolutely necessary (Phillips, 2013). During this golden hour, infant and parent dyads left alone skin to skin will move through a precise series of nine behaviours that ultimately lead to the first breastfeed. These behaviours are:

The First Cry

Often called the birth cry; this helps the baby's lungs to open up.

Relaxation

After a good cry, babies tend to become still and quiet, often gazing around them as they recover from their transition into the world. This is where we often see mothers really begin to explore their baby– stroking their body, looking at their fingers, talking to them gently, etc.

Awakening

A few minutes after birth, the baby will start to move around, often opening and closing their mouth. When left alone, parents will respond with more verbal and physical encouragement.

Activity

This is where the baby will start to look towards the breast. They can see it clearly, thanks to the contrast of the areola against the rest of the mum's skin. They will root, stick out their tongue, and suck their hands. We also often see the baby touch the birthing parent's nipple with their hand and then bring their hand to their mouth.

Rest

These periods of high activity will be interspersed with rest and relaxation throughout the first hour.

Crawling

At around 30-40 minutes after birth, the baby will start to use their feet to push their way up Mum's body to get closer to the breast. They can also lift their head or even their whole torso up away from their parent's body to get to where they need to be for a feed.

Familiarization

Once the baby is nice and close to the breast, they will spend several minutes exploring it. Licking, rooting, and kneading be-haviours are all normal here.

Feeding

About an hour after birth, if left alone with the birthing parent, the golden hour ends with the baby self-attaching and feeding.

Sleep

It's hard work coming into the world! The first feed is followed by an often-deep sleep as the baby rests and the parents continue to familiarise themselves with every inch of their new arrival.

We then see that for these dyads, breastfeeding tends to go better and last longer compared to the mothers and infants who were separated during this time for weighing the baby or other interventions. Parents are often more confident, babies cry less, and we often see there's less nipple pain and problems with infant weight loss. Interrupting this process, even for a few minutes to weigh the baby, can throw the entire dance off track, increasing stress levels for parents and their baby.

Of course, there are times when interruption is needed. For example, if the baby needs to go to the NICU, was born with the birthing parent under general anaesthetic, or if there are problems such as a postpartum haemorrhage. You can recreate the golden hour at a later time and gain many of the same benefits. It isn't quite the same after the first hour, but it can still be an incredibly powerful experience.

Early Feeds

In the first 3-5 days after your baby is born, you'll be asked if breastfeeding is going well. The thing is, you probably don't really know the answer to this. You will have been exposed to conflicting messages about painful feeding while you were pregnant. Some people will have told you that pain is never okay. Others will have said that some pain in the first week is normal. Others still may have shared that they had pain every single day for the first 4 weeks until their nipples toughened up. None of this conflicting advice is helpful when it comes to working out if feeding is going well.

If we had truly excellent breastfeeding support available as standard, I'd like to think that the following would be true in these early days:

- You would have already received consistent messaging from everyone that pain is not normal.

- A trained breastfeeding supporter, which may include a doula, would be available to sit with you for an entire feed, showing you the signs of good feeding and anything you might need to adjust.

- That supporter will be able to come back for the next feed to check if you've figured it out.

- Everyone you have contact with during your maternity care will be *well* trained in breastfeeding support and be able to quickly refer you to an IBCLC or equivalent if there are any signs that you're struggling after some basic changes to positioning and attachment. These people will also have had debriefing around their own infant feeding experiences if they are parents.

I know that some places are excellent at all or most of the above, but it's not consistent, and some hospitals or care providers are missing the mark in a lot of ways. If you're reading this book and preparing to breastfeed your next baby, it can be helpful to do just a little bit of hand expression after a few feeds each day until the baby has been weighed on day 5. This is because it can be hard to be confident in how well your baby is feeding, especially if you're a bit anxious or your nipples are sore. You can either feed your baby the milk you hand express in a little cup, or you can pop it in the fridge in case it's needed later. This extra stimulation is a good way to encourage your milk supply to grow if your baby might not be feeding as effectively as is ideal. I can't change the system, but tips like this can help you to reach your goals in a world that isn't really getting it.

The First Weeks

Once your milk comes in around days 3 to 5 and once your baby has been weighed around day 5, everyone tends to fade into the background a bit more. Unless your baby has lost too much weight, in which case you will find yourself surrounded by a range of opinions and suggestions, often conflicting with each other and all focused on whether *you* can meet your baby's needs. If the baby hasn't gotten back to birth weight by around week 2, parents are often told that their baby isn't taking or getting enough milk. This is likely true, but the wording can lead the parents to feel that the issue is milk supply, not the baby struggling to remove what's available. These issues tend to coincide with the partner needing to return to work, and the novelty of a newborn wearing off for friends and family who were so keen to visit during the first 2 weeks. Mothers are left alone, worried about their milk supply, worried about their baby, told to pump, top up, and latch, all with little to no practical support to achieve this challenging triple feeding expectation.

In an ideal, parent-and-baby-friendly world, partners would have longer parental leave. Studies from 2010 and 2020 noted that a longer duration of shared parental leave was one factor in longer-term breastfeeding (Flacking, Dykes, & Ewald, 2010; Grandahl, Stern, & Funkquist, 2020).

While I'm writing this book from my perspective here in the UK, where we have good maternity leave benefits, I am aware that, in the US in particular, these rights do not exist. This is another barrier to successful breastfeeding that is well documented. Just to touch on this topic, a 2018 review of the available literature concluded that longer maternity leave was clearly associated with longer duration of breastfeeding (Navarro-Rosenblatt & Garmendia, 2018).

As well as better parental leave for both partners, in-home support is also an important factor, not just for meeting your breastfeeding goals, but for parental confidence and wellbeing during the transition into parenthood. For example, in the Netherlands, you could expect to be supported in the first 10 days after having your baby by a service called Kraamzorg. This is where a trained nurse (usually the same person each visit) comes to your home and helps you with baby care, feeding, and your postnatal recovery. In the UK and many other Western countries, we don't have standardized access to this level of support. We can hire a postnatal doula, though, assuming that option is affordable. Doulas are associated with a host of positive outcomes, including those related to breastfeeding. A 2021 review concluded that, as long as the doula has lactation training themselves, they are strongly associated with positive breastfeeding outcomes (Acquaye & Spatz, 2021).

On the topic of postnatal support, another thing a parent needs to have easier access is highly skilled lactation support. An IBCLC or equivalent can have significant positive outcomes on breastfeeding rates (Haase, Brennan, & Wagner, 2019), but in many countries, including the UK, they are not provided as standard. As a result, these professionals work in private practice and charge parents for their work.

The Dutch model of Kraamzorg, the documented benefits of doula access, and the proven positive outcomes from IBCLC support all suggest that in the ideal breastfeeding-friendly world, we would all have access to some sort of daily, well-informed, in-home postnatal support, and highly qualified specialist guidance when needed. As it stands, we don't, and those who need this support most (first-time parents, parents with lower incomes, and those with additional needs) are those who typically find it hardest to access. Is any of this the fault of the family? No. It's a clear indication of a society and/or government that does not value postnatal care, and as a result, is letting down parents and their babies at a time when they need the most support.

In the Health Care System

Go to your GP with a breastfeeding problem and you will usually come away with drugs or instructions to stop breastfeeding. I'm not blaming the GP! This is (yet again) due to lack of training on the topic of lactation and not having enough time to give you the support you need. It's commonplace to believe that doctors are well trained in breastfeeding, but unfortunately, they are not. This is clearly shown in a small 2018 survey, where 58.8% of doctors surveyed believed that infants need cow's milk or formula at 6 months, and only 67% believed that breastfeeding should be responsive, not on a schedule (Shaw & Devgan, 2018). Another survey in 2020 discovered that only 3% of medical students felt confident in assisting parents with latching their babies (Biggs, Fidler, Shenker, & Brown, 2020). Sadly, there is no formal lactation training for doctors and other healthcare students in the UK, with my medically trained friends and colleagues reporting only attending a single 1-hour lecture on the topic during their medical school training.

One of the most common ways GPs can negatively impact breastfeeding is when they incorrectly tell someone to stop breastfeeding in order to take medication. The reason they do this is linked to the inserts that come with drugs typically stating that the medicine is not to be used during lactation. However, these inserts are rarely based on clinical evidence of harm, simply because it's unethical to test drugs on lactating mothers and their little ones. If we take some time to understand how drugs may or may not pass into human milk, though, it quickly becomes clear that most of the time there's no real need to cease breastfeeding to take prescription drugs, and when they *are* contraindicated, there is usually a safer breastfeeding option to consider. In the UK, the Drugs in Breastmilk Information Service is working hard to share accurate information with doctors and parents, allowing mums to continue breastfeeding confidently while taking medications. This service is free, and easily accessible, but as is often the case, you need to know it exists before you can use it.

When we consider that your GP is usually the first place to go when having problems with breastfeeding, this lack of training and knowledge is concerning, and absolutely having a negative impact on mothers trying to reach their breastfeeding goals.

In the UK, we also have access to Health Visitors (HV). These are nurses or midwives who have received additional training to offer universal support to families from birth to 5 years. One of the areas a HV will focus on is infant feeding, including an emphasis on breastfeeding support. Many mothers stop breastfeeding at around the time HVs carry out their second postnatal visit at 6 weeks, which suggests that something about the support being offered by HV services isn't quite as good as it could be. This is unlikely to be the fault of any individual HV, since they are dealing with increased caseloads and reduced funding all over the UK (Bryar et al., 2017). Recent studies show us that around 25% of families aren't getting the contact from their HV that they should be, and this may well be linked to the 16% increase in caseloads that HVs are trying to juggle (Health Visitors Service Delivery Metrics). On top of this, 78% of HVs reported an increase in stress and burnout levels in a 2023 survey carried out by the Institute of Health Visiting. In this same survey, 48% of respondents said they were planning to leave the profession within 5 years, with 94% reporting caseloads way over and above what they should be (Devereux, 2023).

In addition to all of the above, the way that HVs are trained to give breastfeeding support may not be particularly helpful. It's well documented at this point that breastfeeding support works best when it's based in emotional support, but due to high workloads and limited time, alongside the way they are trained, HVs tend to give practical, technical support, with a focus on discussing the benefits of breastfeeding. Several systematic reviews have pointed out that this isn't a good way to increase breastfeeding rates after the initial initiation period. In fact, 80% of parents reported having a harder time breastfeeding when support was focused on information giving rather than connection and emotional support (Giannì et al., 2020). Finally, a 2022 study looked at outcomes for breastfeeding families according to the sort of support the HV gave them; the highest rates of stopping breastfeeding early were clearly linked to those mothers who felt that their HV gave more informational support than emotional (Chambers, Myers, Emmott, & Page, 2022).

You might be wondering about IBCLCs. It often surprises people to learn that the NHS do not routinely employ these experts in infant feeding. In fact, look at a job description for an infant feeding coordinator in a hospital's maternity unit, and they will state that a midwifery qualification is essential. They might state IBCLC is desirable, but often, this qualification isn't mentioned or even taken into consideration when reviewing applications. This is despite there being clear evidence that IBCLC level support helps more people to meet their infant feeding goals (Patel & Patel, 2015).

Essentially, the way the health system is currently funded and run means that families are being seriously let down in many areas, and one of the biggest let downs is breastfeeding support. Your GP is likely to give you inaccurate information and your HV is probably so busy dealing with safeguarding cases that they simply don't have the time to offer the emotional support that we know is more helpful for breastfeeding success. None of this is the individual practitioner's fault, and it certainly is not the fault of the mothers who are turning to these services expecting good support.

In Society

Whenever I'm in an airport, I can't help but notice that most of them use an image of a feeding bottle to represent the baby changing and feeding space. This is one of many indications that we live in a society that has normalised bottles; they are associated so much with babies and how babies are fed, that a bottle is universally recognised as the sign for "baby room." We also see this on New Baby congratulations cards, baby shower decorations, and for adverts aimed at parents with babies. Does it matter? In the grand scheme of things, images of bottles aren't the biggest issue to get worked up about, but the underlying message is that bottles are normal and expected, and *that* is a problem when we're looking at why mothers don't reach their breastfeeding goals.

Many mothers report feeling judged or criticised for breast-feeding, especially beyond 6 months, or if they feed their baby in public. Accusations range from "she's only doing it for her own benefit" to "Is she a paedophile?" and a broad range in between (Newman & Williamson, 2018).

Next, we need to think about how failing to breastfeed leads to very real grief, trauma, and anger that can make seeing anything relating to it feel like an attack. Posters promoting breastfeeding, or images of a breastfeeding mother as the symbol for a baby care room can reinstate your own feelings of shame or disappointment around not breastfeeding. This can and does lead to women being vocal with companies about shaming formula use, and the fear of receiving this anger will often be enough to stop companies depicting breastfeeding in promotional or informational materials.

When we also consider that 27% of Americans think it's embarrassing to see someone breastfeed in public, and a further 31% believe you shouldn't breastfeed a 1-year-old (Li, Fridinger, & Grummer-Strawn, 2002), along with the public opinion in the UK that breastfeeding beyond infancy is lazy and exhibitionist (Grant, 2016), it's of absolutely no surprise to me that bottles are the universal sign for baby. Companies risk being on the receiving end of that stigma if they are seen to promote breastfeeding, not to mention the chances that the people designing these logos and products will likely have their own negative experiences around breastfeeding.

Now, your feelings around bottles and the experience you had breastfeeding may not completely correlate with the above, but let me share with you what a truly breastfeeding-friendly society could look like:

- You wouldn't **ever** be asked to move or use a cover for breastfeeding.
- Dolls wouldn't come with bottles.
- The international sign for baby wouldn't be a bottle.
- There wouldn't be adverts for formula on the TV.
- You wouldn't be asked how well your baby sleeps.
- There would be better paid maternity leave around the world.

- Lactation friendly spaces would be standard.

- You would be able to quickly and easily access excellent but informal breastfeeding support from other mothers in your community.

- You wouldn't be asked how long you're going to breastfeed for.

- Formula wouldn't be suggested if you express that you're feeling tired/depressed /isolated.

- In short, a breastfeeding-friendly society helps parents to breastfeed if they want to. Ours is not doing that.

A Breastfeeding-Friendly Society Also Supports Formula Feeding

We can't pretend that you get buckets of support if you're formula feeding, either. So, you might be wondering how a breastfeeding-friendly world would impact those who choose or need to use formula. I believe that the answer is that someone using formula would receive less judgement, have more support to deal with their feelings, and have access to formula that is more affordable and probably more advanced than the products available today. Here's why I think this would be the case:

- If everyone was suitably well supported in their attempts to breastfeed, then there would be no suggestion that you didn't try hard enough when breastfeeding doesn't work for you.

- Choosing to formula feed would be a truly informed choice, based on accurate information and personal circumstance, further reducing assumptions and judgement from others.

- If the emotions commonly experienced around breast-feeding failure where acknowledged, understood, and considered expected, then there would be support for processing and moving through those feelings when they come up.

- If you're supported to come to terms with your feelings, you are less likely to feel angry, defensive, or triggered when someone else breastfeeds or overcomes a breast-feeding challenge that you couldn't, making it easier for you to support that person, and for them to feel supported.

- If formula companies couldn't spend money on adver-tising, they wouldn't need to charge as much for their products.

- A society that understands the flaws of formula would push for it to be improved, forcing the manufacturers to actually do so (again, instead of spending profits on marketing).

CHAPTER FOUR

How We Got to This Point

While I have explored the history of infant feeding in both *Mixed Up* and *Breastfeeding Myths*, it's so important when we're considering today's breastfeeding rates (and why people don't reach their goals) that I need to talk about this topic here as well.

Before Formula

We know that prehistoric children received breastmilk until around age 2. We have this information from, amongst other things, looking at the age gaps between siblings. Lactation will usually stop your periods from returning, meaning there will be larger age gaps between one child and the next.

However, there is evidence of babies being fed away from their parent's breast throughout history. We have infant feeding devices from ancient Egypt, for example. In ancient Rome, breastmilk was considered important, but may have come from a wet nurse if the mother was of higher standing or couldn't breastfeed herself. Another reason for using a wet nurse was to feed abandoned babies, who were "rescued" and cared for until they were old enough to be used as slaves. Wet nursing was considered a noble profession, and we even have contracts from that time that lay out strict criteria for the wet nurse's payment, which would include not only money, but practical items, such as lamp oil and a clothing allowance (Stevens, Patrick, & Pickler, 2009).

While hiring a wet nurse became something of a status symbol later, they were previously used out of necessity. The earliest known medical encyclopaedia was written in Egypt in around 1550 BCE, and it talks about lactation failure.

By the Middle Ages, wet nursing was still common but becoming more frowned upon. Breastmilk was thought to hold magical properties that could pass on the characteristics of the nurse or mother to the infant. This led to a return of society placing huge importance on a mother breastfeeding her own baby. Of course, this didn't apply to royalty. A queen or lady of high standing needed to become fertile as quickly as possible to produce more heirs. This meant that breastfeeding wasn't ideal, as it would delay the return of her fertility. It was very much expected that a wet nurse would be carefully chosen and employed to feed wealthy babies. It was even recommended that the wet nurse not have red hair, because her fiery temperament could be passed on to the baby through her milk (Wickes, 1953).

What is especially important to note, given the topic of this book, is that while wet nursing was controversial during this time period, it was still recommended and used when a mother was unable to breastfeed. In short, the battle to succeed at lactation is as old as humankind. Yes, we are currently in something of an epidemic of parents not meeting their goals due to society and the influence of formula marketing, but breastfeeding has never been perfect, and we've always relied on the support of other women when things don't work.

In the 19th century, wet nursing as it once was came to an end, as the availability of alternative milks and feeding devices became wider spread. Before this time, using feeding devices was incredibly risky as they would be made from wood, animal bone, pewter, or other components which were hard to clean. It was only a matter of time before the build-up of bacteria made the baby sick, and without modern healthcare, the result was often death. The 19th century feeding bottles were made of glass, which was a lot easier to keep clean. Unfortunately, in the first part of the century, cleanliness wasn't understood well, and the bottles were not typically kept clean–the end result sadly being the same as before, and around one third of babies not breastfed died (Wickes, 1953d).

It would be insensitive of me to not pause here and discuss the long-term negative effects that forced wet nursing had on Black slaves. During the transatlantic slave trade, it was common for slaves to have to feed the babies of the slave owner. This period of time has impacted the experiences and feelings of Black women for generations, making breastfeeding even more challenging for many. I encourage you to read the voices of Black women on this topic. There are many fantastic articles online, shared originally for Black Breastfeeding Week.

Feeding methods aside, around the time of the industrial revolution and particularly in the 1800s, there was a big shift in general birthing and parenting practices, sadly to the detriment of mothers and babies. Hospital birth became expected, with babies taken to a nursery after birth, only being returned to feed on whatever schedule the doctor had decided was appropriate at the time. Mothers were taught to stop sleeping in the same room as their infants for fear of "dirty air" causing illness or death, and childcare experts (always men) laid out feeding and sleeping schedules that typically led to a reduced milk supply. There was a real fear at various points through history that you could spoil a baby by feeding on demand. Of course, what we now know is that limiting breastfeeds is an effective way to reduce milk supply. During the same time period, a new "miracle food" was being feverishly worked on, which would rescue mothers from the "mystery" of their low milk supply.

Formula – A Miracle Food

Enter formula milk! An important invention that has saved countless lives. People needed a solution to the breastfeeding problems they were having due to schedules and routines being forced upon them and their babies. Wet nursing was something that worried people, and feeding them animal milk or soaked bread led to babies dying. Formula absolutely saved (and still saves) more lives than we can begin to guess.

While Henri Nestle is often credited with the invention of formula, it was actually a man called Justus von Liebig who designed and patented the first liquid and powdered milk designed specifically for infants. It was made of cow's milk, wheat and malt flours, and potassium bicarbonate. It was almost immediately decided that this new food was perfect for babies (Radbill, 1981). By the late 1800s, there were several products made by different companies, all claiming to be the best breastmilk substitute.

Lining the Pockets of Formula Companies

Sadly, the lifesaving potential of formula milk was in the wrong hands. Companies wanted to profit from selling their product to as many people as possible, regardless of whether it was really needed. Combine this with a lack of advertising standards in the 19th and early 20th centuries and it's not at all surprising that soon breastfeeding was declining, and more and more babies were having formula milk. The companies would market their formula directly to doctors, who would then recommend it to parents. At one point in time, formula was considered *better* than breast-milk because it was scientifically made. What should have been a medical intervention for when breastfeeding wasn't possible quickly became the standard way to feed babies.

Once you're bottle feeding, you can overfeed. An overfed baby will sleep longer than a breastfed baby. This was helpful in a world where it was believed that you could spoil an infant by responding to their cries, that they *should* sleep for several hours at night, and that if you roomed in with them you might make them sick from your "stale air." Unfortunately for today's parents, this expectation that a baby will sleep "well" and feed no more than every 3 hours is still prevalent in our modern society, even though they are beliefs based on infants being somewhat stuffed full of formula and then left to cry in a room alone. If your baby wants to feed every 2 hours around the clock, you won't have to look further than Instagram to find people telling you how to reduce their feeding and make them sleep longer, against your baby's instincts and very real needs. You will be made to feel like you are not being firm enough, that your milk isn't good enough, or that your baby is manipulating you.

The Nestle Scandal

I mentioned Henri Nestle above, but he also gets an entire section dedicated to the company he formed. The Nestle Scandal is an incredibly important part of history that we need to explore to further understand how companies such as Nestle are actively preventing people from reaching their breastfeeding goals even today.

According to Gabrielle Palmer's book *The Politics of Breast-feeding* in the early 1970s, 87% of mothers in Nigeria were using formula because they thought a nurse had told them they should. These "nurses" were actually saleswomen wearing a uniform that looked similar to that of a nurse. Guess who employed these saleswomen? A formula company (Palmer, 2015, p. 238).

Why does this matter? In short, heavy and unethical marketing practices in developing countries was leading to the death of a lot of babies. This is because the mothers living in the countries targeted didn't have access to clean water, a way to heat the water for washing bottles or preparing the formula, or the funds to continue buying formula after the sales reps successfully got them to stop breastfeeding with free samples. It's currently believed that 66,000 babies died in 1981 alone as a direct result of the marketing strategies being used (Anttila-Hughes et al., 2018).

The WHO Code

As a result of so many babies suffering, the World Health Organisation stepped in and created their Code for the Marketing of Breastmilk Substitutes (commonly just called "the Code"). The Code is aimed at manufacturers, healthcare providers, and shops that sell products covered by it. The Code requests that:

- Formula advertising is factual.
- Items covered by the Code do not come with incentives, such as discount codes or freebies.
- Healthcare workers do not accept gifts, training, or funding from formula companies.

People often zone in on the second point, especially when they realise they can't claim reward card points for formula. It's often felt that this is to penalise formula feeding families, but this isn't the case. We know that when money off or freebies are offered, the companies will ultimately increase the price of their product to claim back the lost costs. By banning coupons, codes, points, and freebies, the WHO is ultimately protecting formula-fed babies by ensuring products are more affordable.

Unfortunately, signing up to the Code is optional. The U.S. doesn't follow it at all, and the UK only follows part of it. This means that in both countries, we are still victim to unethical marketing practices, and this is still having a direct impact on breastfeeding success. Parents offered free samples or money off codes for formula are far less likely to reach their breastfeeding goals (Lisi, de Freitas, & Barros, 2021). The governments know this, but they choose to not uphold the Code. It's not *your* fault if you stopped breastfeeding after receiving free formula; the risks are well known by those in charge of policy making. But at the end of the day, there is more profit to be made in formula feeding.

CHAPTER FIVE

Common Situations That Lead to Feelings of Failure

While I can't cover every single scenario in this book, I did want to take some time to explore the most common reasons for ending breastfeeding early, and why it isn't your fault if this happened to you. You may have experienced none of these situations, or you may have dealt with a combination of several.

Birth Interventions

It's common to be told that if you have a C-section, or certain medication in labour, your baby might be sleepy, slow to latch, and/or your milk might come in a little later than the norm. There are a few reasons for this, but ultimately, in these cases, and particularly where labour was induced or if synthetic oxytocin was given to expel your uterus, we are dealing with a situation where the body has taken the sudden surge in what it perceives to be oxytocin as a sign to slow down its own production of this hormone. Oxytocin is crucial to lactation success. When your baby goes to the breast, it's a surge of oxytocin that makes your milk flow. If your body isn't making that oxytocin, your milk isn't going to flow as well or as quickly, which might lead to a fussy, irritated baby who won't feed. If this experience is repeated for a few days, you may find your baby is slow to gain weight, and that the ongoing problems getting them to remove milk means that your supply reduces. Typically, you will then need to top up (often with formula) and this can quickly take you into "bottle preference" territory, which can further reduce milk supply.

There's another way your birth experience and oxytocin can cause problems, and that's trauma. Oxytocin is a hormone that is released when we feel relaxed and safe. If every time you feed your baby, you have flashbacks to the birth, or every time they latch your nipple feels like it's going to be chewed off, you are not going to be releasing much oxytocin. Then, your baby is probably going to fuss, pull off the breast, and act unsettled. Over time, this entire experience can condition you to associate breastfeeding with pain (physical or emotional) and tension, which will continue to inhibit oxytocin, and therefore, your flow of milk. If it goes on long enough, it can even reduce milk supply, leading to you stopping breastfeeding before you want to.

Prematurity

While there is often a push to provide premature babies with human milk, the way this milk is delivered typically gets less consideration. If you have a preemie, it's likely that you will start out expressing your milk for your baby, and then need to help them to transition to at-breast feeding once they are a little older and developmentally ready to feed. Maintaining a milk supply with a breast pump is tricky; helping a premature infant to breastfeed is tricky; going home with your vulnerable baby from the NICU where you had 24/7 support to suddenly having little to no support is challenging. Often, these babies aren't the best at breastfeeding;

they may have less strength and less coordination when it comes to their suck, swallow, breathe pattern. If they've been intubated, they may have a narrow palate, which makes latching harder, and they will often be sent home taking some volume of supplement or fortifier, meaning that they are being exposed to bottles (and often formula) daily. You might find your baby falls asleep at the breast, latching may be painful, you might need to top up to help them maintain their weight gain, and you might need to pump to support your own supply. All of this happens in addition to caring for a baby who may still require oxygen supplements and/or have other additional needs to support their care. In such a scenario, breastfeeding is something that takes up a lot of time and may not be particularly easy or rewarding for you or your baby. You might find that you reach a breaking point where the *only* thing you can change is breastfeeding.

The issue can then quickly feel like a "how hard are you willing to try" situation. You, the lactating parent, are given the burden of continuing to provide human milk, and if you don't you may feel or be told that you have failed or given up, or that breastfeeding wasn't important enough to you.

Of course, all of the above is in the context of our society. My ultimate question here is how and when did it become normal to not provide the higher levels of personalised support to NICU families after discharge from hospital? If we consider that question rather than asking how much mothers and parents can/should breastfeed or how much they want to, we find ourselves in a different place entirely. Is it *your* fault that triple feeding a high needs or medically complex baby was too much for you to take on? Or is this once again down to a systematic failure to support infants and families?

Slow Weight Gain

This is an incredibly common issue, and one that typically leads to the use of formula. The usual cause of slow weight gain is the baby not removing milk often enough or well enough from the breast. The particular reasons for this are many and include a sleepy baby, a feeding routine, pacifier use, a baby that can't latch well due to oral challenges, muscle tension, a high palate, or Mum's nipples being flat or large. These challenges are often missed in the crucial first days of life when milk supply is being primed, and then the breasts make less milk in response to this reduced stimulation. This then leads you into a tailspin of slow weight gain, instruction to top up, overfeeding with a bottle or bottle preference, even less breast stimulation and, ultimately, even lower milk supply.

Let's read Bex's experience and then explore how she didn't fail but *was* failed.

"My daughter was born in 2015. I had pethidine during labour and as soon as she was born, she fell asleep. I had no clue about how breastfeeding worked. I figured the baby cried and I just stuck a nipple in her mouth - but she didn't cry. The midwives left me and my partner alone for about 3 hours and when they came back they tried to get my daughter to latch, but she wouldn't stay awake, even if we stripped her off. One of them made a comment about it being 'common for pethidine babies to sleep a lot'. I spent the next 24 hours on the ward for 'breastfeeding support' and every 3 hours someone came to help me feed her. Eventually a concerned midwife came and got me to express to cup feed her. I think she said something about that she wasn't supposed to suggest cup feeding, but she was worried my daughter hadn't really fed in about 12 hours.

"I went home the next day and my daughter just slept and slept. My boobs got sore and engorged, so when she did try to feed she couldn't latch properly. I got sore nipples. On day 3 she 'woke up' and was miserable. We called the midwives at 3am because she would not stop crying and I was in floods of tears. They said something about 'pethidine normally affects babies this way'.

"When the midwives weighed her, she had lost 11% of her birth weight and I was told she looked a bit jaundiced. The midwife said we needed to top up with formula 'or else we would have a very sick baby on our hands'. I was devastated, feeling like a failure, but followed the advice I was given.

"My breastfeeding support worker came out and watched me struggle to feed. She couldn't really help. I told her I thought my milk was drying up as I couldn't hand express milk anymore. She tried and couldn't express any either. So I ordered an electric pump which arrived the next day.

"By day 7, my daughter was 100% bottle fed on a combination of breast milk and formula, as I was an under supplier. I would pump for 30 minutes every 3/4 hours. I pretty much became a recluse as I couldn't go far from my pump. At her 6 week check I asked for my daughter to be checked for a tongue tie. The GP confirmed what the midwives, HV and BF support worker had missed. She had one, but they refused to snip it as 'it didn't matter now she was bottle fed'. I developed PND and blamed myself for my daughter's weight loss, mainly because I'd had pethidine in labour. I carried on like this for 9 months until my doctor advised I stopped expressing for the sake of my mental health."

Many mothers in Bex's position will think that their baby didn't want to breastfeed, or that they simply couldn't. There is often a narrative in society of "Well, not all babies take to the breast." However, we can see from Bex's words that because of her persistence in requesting help it ultimately became clear that her baby had a tongue tie. In an ideal world, here is the support Bex would have had access to:

- Breastfeeding lessons in pregnancy. Free and accessible to her in the way that she preferred.

- Antenatal hand expression so that a sleepy baby has access to Mum's own milk ready to go.

- Support to hand express as soon as it became clear the baby wasn't feeding. We need to prime the breasts within the first 6 hours to avoid long term issues with milk supply.

- Topping the baby up with the hand expressed milk much sooner than the 12-hour point.

- A visit from the infant feeding team on day 3, when the baby was distressed, and nipples were sore.

- A tongue tie assessment also on day 3, when persistent issues were obvious.

- A clear and realistic plan to keep the baby fed and milk flowing while the baby struggled to latch, and the parents were waiting for that tongue tie appointment.

While we can't say for sure how different the outcome would have been for Bex and her baby if these measures were in place, it's not a huge stretch to suggest that she may have managed to give her baby more of her own milk, for longer, and perhaps have reduced the severity of her PND thanks to a less stressful and better supported experience.

We can't blame Bex for not having access to this sort of help; it's the fault of poor government funding, which is a reflection of how society views infant feeding. Bex didn't fail; she was failed.

Jaundice

Jaundice is a common newborn condition which affects between 60% and 90% of infants (Hansen, 2021) and in most cases, it doesn't need anything more than plenty of feeding and time to resolve. However, sometimes jaundice does require treatment, and sometimes it can be due to underfeeding. When this happens, parents often find that they're told the baby must have formula. But if the lactating parent can express enough milk to feed her baby, then the need for formula is simply unnecessary. On top of poor information about the milk a baby needs, jaundiced newborns are often sleepy and difficult to wake to breastfeed. This can play into the narrative mentioned in the previous section that "not all babies take to feeding." Since formula has already been introduced for the jaundice, many parents will decide at this point to stop breastfeeding altogether, seeing breastfeeding (rather than lack of breastfeeding support) as a cause of harm to their baby.

Breastfeeding doesn't cause babies to need jaundice treatment; lack of feeding does. If we taught parents to hand express after a few feeds for the first few days, had skilled support immediately on hand so nipples don't get sore in the first place, and gave parents more time with support workers in those days after delivery, then we'd see far less starvation jaundice. How can we expect brand new parents to take home a tiny newborn with absolutely *no* knowledge of what normal feeding looks and feels like, and with no support around them other than their family and friends, who likely formula fed? No wonder babies are being readmitted.

Those who want to push through are often unsupported in building and maintaining their milk supply while the baby is sleepy, leading to chronic supply challenges and a cycle of topping up with formula until, eventually, the parents reach a breaking point and switch to formula entirely.

Here's my idea of good support for jaundice:

- Hand expression in pregnancy to build a small stash of milk, or at least learn the technique if no colostrum is removed.

- Hand expression after a few feeds a day until milk "comes in" This milk can be saved or fed back to the baby via a cup or syringe.

- Closer care for new parents in the first week. A 1-hour midwife visit every other day isn't enough. We should be considering normalising and making available doula support or similar so that someone trained in newborn behaviour is in the home for several hours *daily* in that first week.

Linzi

"I'm a mum of 2 (7.5 YO and 2.5YO) and I failed to establish BF with both. With my first, I tried everything (lactation consultants, TT snipped, treated for thrush, combi feeding, SNS feeding etc) and eventually gave up. I was so determined with my second and had a feeding consultant work with me from 3rd trimester. We seemed

to start well (first 48 hours) then he would scream at feeding times etc. I was so terrified of failing again that I just kept going (had TT snipped). He seemed to settle around day 4 and I was relieved as he was 'sleepy' and not screaming. The midwife came to do her checks and he had lost weight and she was concerned about his condition (jaundiced, dehydrated etc none of which my private feeding consultant had spotted signs of). She told me we had to go to A&E ASAP. I was terrified and on arrival at hospital, we were told he had to have formula every 2 hours until he was back to birth weight. I asked about donor milk and BF support and was told this wasn't available. I felt I had failed my baby and endangered his life due to my desire to BF. We stayed overnight (I was post CS and in pain but no one on the ward asked how I was or if needed anything). I now see that this was the start of trauma and the following several months I became hyper vigilant around Hugo, couldn't sleep for fear he might stop breathing. I was tearful whenever I fed him formula and couldn't bear to see another mum breastfeeding. I had flashbacks to him being in hospital and kept replaying what might have happened if I hadn't gone to A&E with him. My GP and your book (and therapy) were a lifesaver for me. I also see that I didn't bond as well with him as I would have like as I felt I'd failed him."

Linzi's experience is so common, and you might recognise some parts of it in your own journey. Imagine if Linzi had been given the option of expressing after breastfeeding and giving this milk to her baby instead of formula; how different might Linzi have felt about her capabilities as a mother? Imagine if someone had investigated *why* her baby had lost weight, instead of just having him put on formula every two hours. What might have been discovered? A tongue tie? A latch needing work? A baby needing extra support to wake and feed? Linzi will never know, but she didn't fail; she was failed.

Tongue Tie

Tongue tie has always been a condition faced by dyads. There are stories throughout history of midwives in the Middle Ages keeping a sharp fingernail to detach a tight frenulum (Obladen, 2009). However, as formula became seen as desirable, mothers would quickly stop breastfeeding when faced with pain or the other challenges associated with tongue tie. This led to a period of time where tongue tie stopped being identified and treated in most cases.

We're now living in a time where tongue tie is recognised as a problem, and in many cases, it's treated quickly and doing so tends to lead to positive breastfeeding outcomes (Ramoser et al., 2019). However, not everyone who takes a look in a baby's mouth is skilled in recognising tongue tie. There seems to be a common misconception that if a baby can stick their tongue out, they don't have tongue tie or that a tongue tie is slight and shouldn't cause any problems. When talking with parents, many tell me that a midwife, support worker, or health visitor tell them these things, and the parents believe that this is a tongue tie assessment, and therefore, their issues are not related to a tight or restricted frenulum. In turn, they continue to try and push through pain, slow weight gain, frequent feeding, and even low milk supply, never getting to the bottom of their issues and ultimately stopping breastfeeding exhausted, confused, and disillusioned.

A tongue tie can only be diagnosed and treated by a tongue tie practitioner. This is someone who has had specific training to make such an assessment and to assume responsibility for carrying out what is essentially minor surgery on a baby. Their assessments are in depth and include a thorough examination of how the infant moves their tongue when sucking on the practitioner's finger, how well the tongue can move from side to side, what the palate feels like, and how tight the lingual frenulum is (Araujo et al., 2020). None of this can be discovered through observing a baby stick their tongue out, and the only person who can describe the type of tongue tie is the person doing the assessment. In fact, many practitioners argue that there is no such thing as a slight tongue tie – either the frenulum is causing problems or not, and if it's causing problems, then it's a tongue tie.

SIGNS OF TONGUE TIE

- Painful feeding, from early on, despite being taught a range of techniques to improve latching.

- Nipple damage.

- Frequent feeding (often, but not always, with long periods of sleep at night).

- Frequent clicking or smacking noises during all feeds.

- Baby appears to fall off/slip back or lose their latch regularly.

- Slow weight gain.

- Low milk supply.

- No matter what you do, baby can't seem to gape to latch

Oral Dysfunction

While oral dysfunction can be caused by tongue tie, it can also oc-cur due to cranial issues, head pain, or birth injury, in preemies or in babies with genetic disorders. Oral dysfunction just means that something in the mouth isn't working in the way we would expect it to. Perhaps the tongue isn't moving in the best way to remove milk, perhaps the baby can't make a good seal around the breast, or maybe they get tired during feeds and slip off.

Oral dysfunction is rarely explored or even mentioned, and many general professionals don't know what to look for, or how. However, it can often be treated with gentle, consistent exercises, sometimes called suck training.

Sarah

"I had breastfed my first two babies with some normal challenges. So by the time Noah was born I was confident about feeding. It was quite the shock when he just couldn't seem to latch. He would open his mouth and place it around my breast but then just stay still, and look confused. He had a tongue tie, so we got that released on day 5. Then I took him to see a chiropractor three times. The chiro said Noah had a lot of tension around his neck and face, but nothing she did made any difference. By week 2 we stopped cup feeding and I gave Noah expressed milk in bottles for ease. He struggled to form a good seal on the bottle, with milk pouring out the sides of his mouth no matter how slowly I kept the flow.

"I took him to the GP, who was less than interested. Noah was gaining weight well so as far as the doctor was concerned there couldn't be anything that seriously wrong with him. I asked for a referral to Speech and Language and was told there was no need.

"I saw 2 IBCLCs. Both said that Noah's tongue wasn't moving how they expected it to, and that he didn't try to suck their finger into his mouth during their assessments. They both gave me some suck training exercises to do with him and helped me with pumping, but they also said that we really needed to see someone from Speech and Language. I was so stuck. I could see what was needed, but the access to that was denied by the NHS. I kept expressing but with two other children to care for, and Noah being slow to feed even with the bottle, I could only manage 4 pumping sessions a day. Obviously this reduced my milk supply and Noah had about 50% formula from 7 weeks old.

"I finally managed to access a specialist through a friend of a friend. He spent a few minutes looking at Noah and found a small hidden cleft palate. This was the cause of all our problems and it had been missed by so many people. I combi fed Noah with expressed breastmilk and formula until he was 6 months old, and then I decided it was time to stop pumping for my mental health and the wellbeing of all of my children. I had wanted to breastfeed for 2 years."

Sarah is describing a submucosal cleft palate in the story above. Fortunately, this is a rare cause of oral dysfunction, and it's unusual for it to be missed. However, it does describe fairly well the difficulties with accessing specialist, multiagency support in regard to infant feeding. It's out of scope for an IBCLC to be looking around for issues like cleft palates and referring to a speech and language therapist (SALT) is absolutely the right move. Unfortunately (in the UK at least), actually getting to see SALT under the NHS can be difficult. This is an example of where bottles were probably masking the underlying condition, as they were allowing Noah to gain weight appropriately. Sarah was obviously not going to let him go without! But the tendency many professionals have in our current system to only look at weight gain as a marker for successful feeding meant that, in this case, Noah went several months with an undiagnosed cleft palate, and Sarah needed to stop breastfeeding much earlier than she wanted. Would earlier diagnosis have meant a different outcome in this case? It's hard to be sure, but it would have opened up some highly specific support for Sarah to access.

Pain

Pain is one of the most common reasons people stop breast-feeding. While this can come with particular feelings of shame ("Why couldn't I just grit my teeth through it?"), it makes sense that there comes a point where someone is just done with every single feed hurting them. Breastfeeding doesn't just happen a few times a day. It can be 10, 12, even 16 times a day, and can last for an hour each time. Pain is a warning sign that something is wrong. Putting yourself through a painful experience multiple times a day, around the clock, and getting no reward for that pain, is likely to end with depression, anxiety, exhaustion, and even fear of feeding. Breastfeeding shouldn't hurt, and painful feeding has a cause. It should *not* be the parent's responsibility to battle their way through pain.

Martha

"The pain started on the second feed. It wasn't too bad to start with, just a bit pinchy. I told the midwife and she said that was normal in the first few days, so I carried on with it. By day 3 my nipples were cracked and bleeding. Someone came to watch us feed and said the latch looked great so maybe I just needed to wait for things to toughen up. Two days later I took baby off after a feed and a piece of my nipple was gone! There was blood in baby's mouth, and he vomited pink—my blood. I decided there and then to stop breastfeeding. I was so afraid I was going to literally have my nipples taken off!

"A few weeks later I was at a baby massage class, talking with another mum. My baby opened his mouth and she audibly gasped. "Look at that tongue tie!" she exclaimed. He had a really obvious line of skin attached to his tongue. No one else had mentioned it to me. This mum told me about how tongue tie *can make feeding painful and recommended I asked the health visitor for an appointment at the local clinic. Two weeks later, I think, 100% tie was snipped, and the worker at the hospital couldn't believe it had been missed.*

"While I'm pleased we got to the bottom of the problems, it was too late for me to breastfeed."

Martha's experience above is far, far too common. She was dismissed from the very first day of breastfeeding. Her damaged nipples were put down to not being tough enough yet, and this continued lack of appropriate support led not only to significant physical trauma to Martha's nipples, but also to the emotional trauma of witnessing that damage and the aftermath of ending breastfeeding before she wanted to. To have a fellow parent notice a tongue tie in a baby group should be mind-blowing, but I've seen it happen more than once in my own life.

Martha didn't fail to breastfeed. She was told that everything was okay by people in positions of trust and authority. Stopping to protect herself from permanent physical damage was the most logical option available to Martha at the time. Could she have attended a support group, hired an IBCLC, or called a helpline? Well, yes. But she should also have been able to trust the professionals telling her there were no problems. It should not fall on the mother, in pain, recovering from birth, exhausted, and navigating the biggest transition of her life, to go out and find support that ought to be immediately and easily accessible as standard.

Frequent Feeding

Nothing prepares you for how often a baby feeds! We are also told to not bedshare with our babies, and to put them down in a safe sleep space for every single sleep. Biologically speaking, we are designed to keep our babies touching us at almost all times. We know this from looking at our milk and comparing it to other species. We are closest to other "carry" species when it comes to milk composition. Carry species milk is quite low in fat because the infant is expected to feed often. For example, human milk holds around 4.5g of fat per 100ml, and many types of primate milk have a fat content of around 5g per 100ml. However, a rabbit has high fat milk (around 13g per 100ml) because they are "cache" animals, meaning they leave their young hidden for many hours, only feeding occasionally.

I am not suggesting we break with safe sleep guidance and blindly bedshare with our babies. However, there is a lot of nuance in the research when it comes to safe sleep practices, and there are many occasions where it can be safe, and certainly safer than accidently falling asleep with the baby on the sofa. For more on safer bedsharing, BASIS online, The Safe Sleep 7 from La Leche League, and The Lullaby Trust are evidence-based resources easily available online.

Let's also remember that many other cultures, and throughout history, there would be more support for new parents, making the frequent breastfeeding easier to handle. In some cultures, for example, you would be confined to bed for around 6 weeks after your baby is born, and women from your family would arrive in the home to keep it running smoothly while also ensuring the mother was well fed, hydrated, and nurtured.

Tasha tells a familiar story that sums up the lack of education and support we are still fighting against. She was denied access to information she needed in order to understand cluster feeding and her options around sleep. The Safe Sleep 7 may have provided some clarity to Tasha and her partner, allowing them to make an informed decision about whether they wanted to set up a bedsharing space or not. A breastfeeding supporter or doula could have spoken about setting alarms or napping in the day. Even if the bottle of formula was decided to be the best option, a peer supporter or other breastfeeding knowledgeable person could have talked through paced bottle feeding and expressing to help Tasha maintain the breastfeeding experience she wanted to have with her baby. Instead, she found herself alone, worried, and presented only with a bottle as the solution, sending her spiralling into the top-up trap.

Tasha

"I knew that babies feed 8–12 times a day. I didn't know that those feeds could be 40 minutes long or close together. I had no idea about cluster feeding and I hadn't considered that my baby would cry if I tried to put her down after feeding.

"I was exhausted by the end of the second week and fell asleep holding her to feed. I woke up quickly and she was safe, thank goodness. But that was when I knew something had to change. I was scared to bedshare because I'd read about the risk of SIDS being higher then. My partner was back to work, driving a tractor, and neither of us wanted him to be tired and risk having an accident.

"A bottle of formula at bedtime seemed to be the best option. I didn't know that I should express to maintain my supply though. After a week, she'd wake about 3 hours after her bottle but just scream at my breast. So I introduced another bottle because I could see she was hungry. I now know this was the start of the top up trap, and the beginning of the end of breastfeeding for us. By the time she was 2 months old she was completely formula fed and I thought it was because I had low milk supply."

Unsupportive Family or Friends

Research has shown us over and over again that a supportive family and surrounding community is so important to breastfeeding success. If you have someone in your home who is asking you if your baby is getting enough from you every time they feed, or saying that *you* were sleeping through the night by 3 days old, or pointing out that if you used bottles other people could help out with feeding, it's going to plant seeds of doubt. At the very least, it's going to be deeply annoying.

If you then find yourself dealing with pain, slow weight gain, fussy feeding, or plain and simple exhaustion, you can then find that you don't have anywhere to turn to for support. The family and friends around you will often shrug and tell you to stop breastfeeding. They may tell you that your mental health is suffering, or that you're martyring yourself to breastfeeding. You will almost certainly hear "fed is best." Many parents with an unsupportive or simply uninterested family report that someone ends up buying them formula against their wishes. Once that formula is in the home, and you're beaten down, it's just a matter of time before it's opened and used.

Breastfeeding Being Blamed When the Parents Struggle

Over the years I have often heard statements such as:

- "They told me if I stopped breastfeeding he would sleep better."
- "My husband felt left out because I was breastfeeding."
- "He was feeding too much, and X person said it was because my milk wasn't good enough."
- "All I did was feed, feed, feed. I couldn't care for my other child."

This is when we see the cracks in modern society where babies, mothers, and marginalised folk are concerned. We often talk about "The Village" in the world of parenting, and you've likely heard this phrase yourself. In case you haven't, The Village is the idea that we aren't supposed to raise children alone or in a couple, but in a community (traditionally, this would often have been a village in the Western world). In some distant past, children would have entertained each other; the older girls would have roleplayed being Mummy with the toddlers, keeping them out of their actual mother's hair. Neighbours would bring over food, do your washing, and generally check in on you after giving birth. In some cultures, and in ancient history, even breastfeeding would have been shared between the lactating women in the community. It was less brutal being awake all night because your preteen niece would love nothing more than to sit and hold your baby while you napped in the day.

In the 21st century, we rarely have anything that even resembles The Village to look out for us when we become a family. If you're lucky, your partner will have a few weeks of parental leave they can take before being forced back to work, leaving Mum at home with a baby that is waking every 2 hours overnight, needs holding nearly all the time, and cries for no obvious reason. On top of this, the parent at home is often still trying to get to grips with breastfeeding, is recovering from a C-section or various other postnatal discomforts, is filled with hormones, and has no idea what her identity is anymore. But wait, there's more. Everyone who was so desperate to come and see the baby in the 2 weeks after it was born has suddenly disappeared, taking their lasagnes and bags of shopping with them. Now we have a new mother and her new baby alone at home, trying to figure out pretty much everything.

There isn't much we can change about newborn behaviour. We can't really force them to sleep in their cot, to fill their nappy less often, or to be happy when put down. But we *can* stop breast-feeding. That is something you might feel you have a degree of choice about, or it might be something that people around you feel they can change on your behalf. You might even be told that your baby will sleep better and that more people could help you if you stopped breastfeeding. Sadly, this is rarely true. So, you stop breastfeeding, your baby still wakes a million times a night, but now they also have reflux from the formula and you're blaming yourself for not carrying on with the breastfeeding.

Grandmothers

It's common knowledge in the infant-feeding world these days that one of the biggest signs someone might breastfeed is if she knows she herself was breastfed (Ekstrom, Widstrom, & Nissen, 2003). While it feels logical to guess that there might a hereditary rea-son for lactation success, such as "good milk making genes," we actually know that it's more likely to do with your mum's attitude to breastfeeding, as well as your experiences of seeing siblings breastfed, seeing your mum's friends breastfeed, and breastfeed-ing being positively talked about growing up. It's also likely that your mother is supportive of breastfeeding if she was successful at it. Most critically, she will know far more about how to support you if she has experience.

If your mother didn't breastfeed, she will likely have parented in a different way to how she might have parented if she did breastfeed. It's more likely she was encouraged to get you into a routine of four hourly feeds and sleeping through the night.

If she tried to breastfeed but ended up stopping early, she will likely also have some pretty complex feelings about feeding.

Unresolved trauma alongside the generally poor breastfeeding knowledge and support in the 80s and early 90s means she probably knows little about what's normal and may see something, such as a fussy period during cluster feeding, as a sign that you aren't making enough milk for your baby, rather than a biologically normal behaviour designed to promote long term milk supply. Unfortunately, we know from the research that your mother is likely to try to stop you from breastfeeding if she thinks it's a bad idea based on her own experience or lack of knowledge (Grassley & Nelms, 2008).

We know this well-intentioned but ultimately misguided approach can make a big difference. Where grandmothers are positive about breastfeeding, a parent is 12% more likely to sustain lactation. However, if the grandmother is negative, this can reduce the chances of someone meeting their lactation goal by up to 70% (Negin et al., 2016). To put it simply, if your mother or mother-in-law doesn't want you to breastfeed, you probably won't breastfeed, at least not for long. Keeping to the topic of this book, this is clearly not a failure on your part. Coming under fire (even well-intentioned fire) from someone you love, trust, and who has close and intimate access to your family unit makes it difficult to hold firm against them. How many comments about cluster feeding being a sign of low milk supply can you listen to before they start to permeate? How many frowns and concerned statements along the lines of "Hmm, I think he's still hungry" when your baby cries after a breastfeed can you hear before concerns from someone older and "wiser" triggers your own anxiety?

Becca

"My Mum was very unhappy with me breastfeeding. Her own failure with me and my brother meant that she was just very suspicious of the whole thing. Every time I fed my baby and she was there, she'd tut and say "He can't be hungry AGAIN?" He was gaining weight perfectly and feeding every two hours most of the time, with some cluster feeding in the afternoon and more feeding if he was tired as well. At one point she even turned up to my house with a tub of formula, telling me I needed it just in case I ran out of milk in the middle of the night. When my baby got to 4 months old and hit the sleep regression, my mum was very worried it was because of my milk supply. Sadly, because I was so exhausted at this point I ended up listening to her and giving some bottles of formula. This was the beginning of the end for my breastfeeding journey as my little one began to prefer the faster flow of the bottle and started to fuss more and more at the breast, making mum point out how much happier he was with a bottle. By 5 months we were exclusively formula feeding. Looking back, there was nothing wrong. He had been gaining weight perfectly, feeding was enjoyable for both of us, and he was just in a sleep regression."

Becca's story above is the perfect example of how a well-meaning grandmother can form a big part of the picture when it comes to doubts around breastfeeding. Becca tells us twice that breastfeeding was going well, but her mother's constant doubts and worries lead to Becca and her baby not reaching their feeding goal.

It's important here to not blame Becca's mum, though. She would have been trying to parent in the UK in the 80s, a time when she would have been encouraged to schedule feeds, introduce solids at 3 or 4 months old, and when nighttime waking was seen as problematic. She almost certainly was actively encouraged to formula feed and get Becca into a routine as fast as possible. Becca's mum is a victim of a formula feeding society as much as Becca and her baby are.

At the same time, it's equally as important to not dismiss Becca's experience for fear of upsetting her mother. Becca was let down by her mum, in the same way her mum was, in turn, let down by the world she lived in. Neither Becca nor her mum failed.

Partners

When we look at studies, partners (where they exist) have a big role to play when it comes to whether their child is breastfed or not. While we know that your partner, if you have one, being supportive of breastfeeding is important, some recent studies have found that the more hands-on a father is with parenting practices, the less likely it is that a baby will be breastfed for longer. The studies specifically talk about fathers, but it's easy to guess that the same would apply to same sex relationships and other forms of close relationships. Things such as getting up in the night to soothe baby so Mum could rest longer tended to lead to less breastfeeding, and it's not a big leap to guess that this might be due to reduced milk supply from skipped feeds, and/or Dad/non-lactating partner giving baby a bottle. However, the same study found that simply having the baby's father in the home increased the chances of breastfeeding getting started in the first place (Emmott & Mace, 2015).

We also know that breastfeeding seems to last longer when your partner comes along to breastfeeding education classes with you or is present while you're getting breastfeeding support. This is probably because, when partners understand the science of breastfeeding, they're more likely to want you to succeed (Mahesh et al., 2018).

While we have made some amazing strides in the attitudes of men and fathers when it comes to parenting and infant feeding over the last generation, it is still far from guaranteed that your baby's father will offer emotional support and attend support or antenatal sessions. I can attest to this myself; it's **very** common for dads to greet me when I arrive at the family home to provide feeding support, and to then disappear, even when actively encouraged to stay. In fact, it's so rare for them to pull up a chair and participate in the support, that when they do, it surprises me.

Writing this section raised my curiosity as to *why* I don't tend to see dads when I'm working, so I asked my social media community to ask their partners about it. The responses I received included:

- Support was given while I was at work.
- I needed to care for our other children.
- I felt uncomfortable with the supporter.
- I wasn't sure what my role would be.
- I didn't want to get in the way.
- I didn't want other women in the peer support group to be uncomfortable.

For those whose partners **did** stay for breastfeeding support, the feeding parents told me that the partners:

- Reminded them later of tips.
- Could see if the feeding position used was the same as when the supporter was there (and help the mum to change her position accordingly).
- Asked insightful questions.
- Felt empowered to be actively supportive (especially if they had been given a role, such as finger feeding, paced bottle feeding, or washing pump parts).

Everyone agreed that a supportive partner was key to their breastfeeding success.

Of course, not everyone has a supportive partner, or a partner at all. While some dads are simply uninvolved with babies and infant feeding, other partners can be openly dismissive of breastfeeding, and even feel jealous of the baby having so much access to their partner's body or worry that breastfeeding will ruin their partner's breasts (García-Fragoso et al., 2013). If you are trying to establish or maintain breastfeeding when the adult you spend most of your time with is either uninterested, unhelpful, or actively critical of what you're doing, it doesn't really require a study to tell us that keeping up the breastfeeding relationship you would like to have is going to be a lot harder. You are already dealing with misinformation from friends and professionals, a society that has normalised bottle feeding, you are not surrounded by "the Village," and you may well be struggling with cluster feeding, pain, or slow weight gain worries. If you're also faced with a lack of support from you closest loved one, it's not your fault if it gets to a point where it's easier to just stop breastfeeding to maintain the peace.

Your Ethnicity

While women in general are being set up to fail breastfeeding, if you have black or brown skin, or if you're from a minority ethnicity, you are also likely to deal with additional barriers to breastfeeding. This often looks like microaggressions. For example, the false narrative in the UK that "black women are better at breastfeeding" might mean that you aren't offered support. Or the belief that "black women are aggressive" might also mean that support staff pull back from offering you help. Once out in the community, simply attending a breastfeeding support group could mean that instead of getting help with feeding your baby, you are asked a series of inappropriate questions including, "Where are you originally from?" or people might randomly touch you or your baby's hair. You might be from a culture where you cannot expose your breast around men, and if dads or male supporters are welcomed at your local breastfeeding support group, this is going to pose an additional risk for you that is often not considered in UK centric support systems.

All of the above essentially means that it can be a lot harder for many people to access lactation support, and when support *is* accessed, it could be culturally inappropriate or racist, making it unhelpful.

A Word on Less Common Situations

While the majority of people will experience the issues mentioned above (or a combination of them), there are of course some less common situations that lead to breastfeeding ending early. Some of these are medical, such as a cancer diagnosis forcing early weaning. Sometimes, they're due to previous emotional trauma (sexual abuse focusing on the breasts, for example) or body dysmorphia. Occasionally, a controlling partner will force someone to stop breastfeeding, either overtly or covertly. Whatever the reason you stopped breastfeeding, it is not your fault. Protecting yourself physically and/or mentally is incredibly important to longer term parenting. If stopping breastfeeding means that you can have the treatment you need, or that you can heal your relationship with your body, then that is a wonderful act of love, not only for your baby's future with you in their life, but for the body you may feel at war with. Keep yourself and your baby safe. You are doing so well.

CHAPTER SIX

Accessing the Support That Should be Standard

This far into the book, you might be wondering how on earth anyone is succeeding at breastfeeding. With appropriate support so desperately lacking for so many dyads, we have to ask the questions; where can you get support currently, and what will that support offer that is different from the standard? Essentially, where can you turn next time if you need more support than is automatically offered?

IBCLC

As an IBCLC (International Board-Certified Lactation Consultant) myself, I'm obviously passionate about this specialised qualification. An IBCLC is the gold standard of training in lactation around the world, and we only focus on lactation and feeding. While some IBCLCs may also be doctors, osteopaths, dentists, nurses, or speech and language specialists, they won't typically merge their hats. If you're seeing someone as an IBCLC, they will only (usually) talk with you about feeding, unless they have insurance that allows them to mix and match their qualifications. Many other IBCLCs have no medical background, instead coming from a breastfeeding volunteer background. These people often have in-depth training around counselling skills from their voluntary work.

Regardless of background, an IBCLC will be well equipped to help you with all things breastfeeding related, especially the more complex situations. They don't work alone, though; research tells us that lactation care is at its best when there is a multiagency approach, which includes, but is far from limited to, an IBCLC.

Osteopath or Chiropractor

While we don't currently have a lot of good research about the difference chiropractors or osteopaths can make to infant feeding, this is mostly because helpful research hasn't been carried out, not because there's no merit to the work (Edwards & Miller, 2019). The most helpful review of the literature I could find concluded that chiropractic care can help babies to breastfeed by working on various skeletal and muscular issues, such as tension in the jaw (Alcantara, Alcantara, & Alcantara, 2015). There also seems to be little risk when it comes to body work for infants (as long as you see an appropriately-trained chiropractor or osteopath). Alongside the apparent low risk, many parents do say that they personally felt body work helped to overcome their breastfeeding issues.

Unfortunately, this lack of evidence means that it's not guaranteed that you'll be told about the potential usefulness of bodywork by a doctor, midwife, or other professional. In some cases, you may even be told not to seek out this support because there's no evidence for it.

Tongue Tie Provider

Some people still claim that tongue tie isn't real. Thankfully, we have numerous studies now that demonstrate the issues tongue tie can cause and how treatment (a frenotomy, where the tie is snipped or lasered away) can make an often immediate and positive change to feeding effectiveness and comfort for the parent (Ghaheri et al., 2017). In the UK, access to a tongue tie provider can be a mixed bag. Some NHS trusts train midwives or employ a tongue tie provider who only assesses and releases ties. In these cases, the waiting list to be seen can be short. Often, the tongue tie is even released while the baby is still in hospital after birth. In other areas, the service can be almost impossible to access with waiting lists of 6 weeks or longer, and (infuriatingly), sometimes the Trust will only snip tongue ties if an infant is under the age of 6 weeks. If we consider that for the first week after birth, you'll likely be told that the issues you're experiencing are due to you and baby learning how to feed, and you might then need to wait 4-6 weeks to get a full tongue tie assessment and release, it quickly becomes impossible to access this support through the NHS. There are of course private practitioners, but the cost of accessing them may be prohibitive for a lot of families, especially if you've been told your baby has a "mild" or "slight" tongue tie, or that having it snipped may not help.

Doula

I love doulas. In fact, I think if the world could have one professional as standard for all life transitions, a doula would be exactly the sort of person who could ease those transitions, reducing the burden and, therefore, poor mental health outcomes on a huge number of people. In regard to the postnatal period, a doula who has some training in breastfeeding support can be the most important person you hire or let into your home. As for breastfeeding alone, one study mentioned in a review of the literature found that 89% of people who hired a doula were still breastfeeding at 6 weeks, compared to 40% of mothers who didn't have doula support (Ramey-Collier et al., 2023). The same review also talks through how families who hire a doula have higher levels of self-esteem postnatally.

Well-Trained Medical Professionals

While we've talked a lot about the professionals who aren't able to support breastfeeding, it is so important that we also take some time to acknowledge those who are *incredible* at supporting it. This might be your own GP, or it might be a particular health visitor or midwife at your local NHS trust (you often hear about these people from other parents). Surround yourself with professionals who understand and support lactation, and you will go far with your journey.

CHAPTER SEVEN

When You Had the Support but Still Didn't Meet Your Goal

Perhaps you're reading this book and genuinely had excellent support. A breastfeeding counsellor mother, for example, or your own in-depth lactation training for your job. You might be thinking "I *had* access to all of that stuff, and I *still* didn't manage to meet my breastfeeding goal! What about me?" This chapter is for you.

First of all, you are not the first person throughout history to find breastfeeding hard, despite living in a supportive environment. We have had wet nurses and infant feeding devices all the way through human history for a reason, after all.

I mentioned earlier that failed lactation is mentioned in the earliest medical encyclopaedia (called *The Papyrus Ebers*), which was written in Egypt at around 1550 BCE. It even has a prescription for lactation failure:

"To get a supply of milk in a woman's breast for suckling a child: Warm the bones of a swordfish in oil and rub her back with it. Or: Let the woman sit cross-legged and eat fragrant bread of soused durra, while rubbing the parts with the poppy plant" (Wickes, 1953, p. 154).

Having this recommendation in writing strongly suggests that an inability to breastfeed was a genuine concern in ancient Egypt. We know that the Egyptians considered lactation to be so important that it was almost magical, and if you were a royal wetnurse, you would expect to be given a huge number of privileges, including a large tomb after your death, and statues, carvings, and artwork showing you and the royal child you nursed. There seemed to be few career options for women in ancient Egypt but wet nursing is portrayed in a way that suggests that this was an exception, and an honour. Even those wet nursing for non-royals would expect to be paid and to work to a contract (Yee, 2009).

What does this have to do with someone not meeting their breastfeeding goals today? The ancient Egyptians considered human milk to be incredibly valuable, and *still*, they needed wetnurses. We see this repeated throughout history as well. Yes, royalty have always used wetnurses, but so have the common people when they weren't able to breastfeed their children themselves. Remember, too, that these were societies where breastfeeding was much essential for infant survival, and it was very much the normal and done thing. Sometimes, we fail to meet a breastfeeding goal, not because society let us down, but because something isn't working for either the parent or the baby. These aren't your fault any more than falling into a topping up cycle is the fault of the parents. Let's look at some of these reasons now.

Some reasons you might not have met your goal

Hypoplasia

Breast hypoplasia (sometimes called insufficient glandular tissue) is where your breasts have less milk making tissue than is ideal for lactation. For some people, this can be pronounced, making producing a milk supply nearly impossible. For others, it can be subtle, with the parents struggling to make a full supply of milk. We don't have consistent data on how common hypoplasia is, at least in part because it tends to go undiagnosed, but signs can include widely spaced, narrow breasts. The good news is that your breasts lay down more milk-making tissue with each pregnancy, so if you couldn't breastfeed your first baby, you may be able to breastfeed in the future.

PCOS

Polycystic ovary syndrome can cause low milk supply in some cases. This might be because someone with PCOS may have less breast tissue, but it might also be related to insulin resistance or other hormonal differences seen across the PCOS spectrum (Britz & Henry, 2011). PCOS doesn't have a known cause, but it seems to be linked to unusual hormone levels, and it does have a genetic association (Ajmal, Khan, & Shaikh, 2019).

Thyroid Disorder

Your thyroid is a gland in your neck, which sends out prolactin and oxytocin– two critical hormones for lactation. Problems can occur when the thyroid makes too much or not enough of something called thyroid hormone. Symptoms, postnatally, are often dismissed as the baby blues or normal new parent exhaustion.

Given that these symptoms are typically anxiety, weight loss or gain, exhaustion, forgetfulness and difficulty sleeping, it's somewhat understandable that thyroid disorder may be missed at first. Thyroid disorder can be caused by inflammation of the thyroid, iodine deficiency, an autoimmune disease, childbirth, or it can be something you're born with. The good news is that, once identified and appropriately medicated, low milk supply caused by thyroid problems will often increase if you are taking proactive steps, such as frequent pumping or latching.

Damage or Surgery to Yours Breasts/Chest Area

When you have surgery on your breasts, there are some risks for your future lactation goals. These risks include:

- Milk-making tissue being removed
- Nerve damage
- Scar tissue
- Increased pain
- The type of surgery carried out (for example, an incision made around the areola is far more likely to cause problems than one under the breast tissue)
- Recent surgery is more likely to cause problems than older ones

Breast or chest surgery is valid. I want to be clear on that. Even if the surgery you had was for cosmetic reasons, this suggests that your mental health and/or self-esteem were negatively impacted by how your breasts looked before. You may have been told at the time that breastfeeding wouldn't be a problem, or it may simply be that when you had your surgery, you didn't think about/ care about the possibility of some future hypothetical lactation. It's normal and okay for priorities to change. I know some of you reading this will be blaming yourself for having cosmetic surgery, regardless of what I say, but I hope you will let me hold the belief for you until you're able.

Of course, there are other reasons for this type of surgery, which is not limited to breast cancer, back pain from large breasts, or gender-affirming care. Let's not spread the narrative that we should put our own health or comfort to one side in case we decide to breastfeed in 5-, 10-, or 15-years' time. Breastfeeding is something we do for a few years, at the most. We have to live in our bodies for decades, and being healthy and comfortable reduces the risk of depression and suicide, apart from anything else (von Soest, Kvalem, Skolleborg, & Roald, 2011; Akhavan, Sandhu, Ndem, & Ogunleye, 2021).

DMER

Dysphoric Milk Ejection reflex is a condition where your milk letting down causes a rage of physical and emotional sensations that are, at best, uncomfortable, and, at worst, unbearable. These symptoms include nausea, depression, "homesickness," anger, and anxiety. It seems to be linked to hormonal changes in your body as your milk begins to flow, and while there are some things you can do to manage your symptoms, you can't stop them completely. DMER is incredibly challenging to experience, and it may reach a point where you are dreading feeds so much, that continuing to breastfeed is simply not good for your mental wellbeing.

Oral Issues for Baby

We talked about oral dysfunction and tongue tie earlier in this book. These issues can lead to low milk supply over time, and low milk supply can make feeding even harder for your baby, meaning supply reduces further and you end up having to give supplements or stop breastfeeding altogether. This is especially likely if you haven't been given access to professionals who understand that your baby might be having difficulties feeding and just tell you that you're not making enough milk.

You're Neurodivergent

As a neurodivergent mother, the first thing that comes to my mind when I think about how neurotypes such as autism or ADHD can lead to someone stopping breastfeeding is the sensory overwhelm. If you're hypersensitive to touch or sensations, that is potentially going to make breastfeeding an overwhelming experience at times. I only have to say "nipple twiddling" to make a room of breastfeeding parents wince. If you have sensory differences, *everything* related to feeding can feel like that nails-on-a-chalkboard experience of a nipple twiddling toddler. Maybe you can't stand the feel of your wet bra or breast pad after you leaked milk. Maybe flutter feeding (fast, light sucks) puts you on edge. Perhaps you can feel your letdown and it makes you want to scream. These are just a few examples of how the sensory experience of lactation can be a lot for someone who is neurodivergent. There are many more considerations worth a book of their own. But let's not forget the stress, confusion, and anxiety that might come up with an unpredictable baby when your life has been carefully structured to allow you to function. While many neurodivergent people do find breastfeeding to be easier and less stressful than formula feeding, there are also many who have the opposite experience. It's important to consider the potential problems that can come up for neurodivergent people when forced to deal with situations that dysregulate them on a daily (or hourly) basis. Depression, anxiety, trauma, and burnout as a result of constant exposure to overwhelming experiences are real and can lead to poorer outcomes for the baby, as well as the parent (whether you're neurodivergent or neurotypical).

You Experience Gender or Body Dysphoria

Not everyone who lactates for their baby identifies with being a woman. Others have experienced abuse or trauma leading to viewing or touching their breasts or chest to feel distressing. Both of these situations can make feeding your baby with your own body a deeply challenging experience. Having feelings of disgust, sadness, confusion, or shame come up every time you need to feed your baby sounds like a recipe for stopping before you really want to, and even being traumatised. We talked in Chapter One about the definition for trauma, and at that time, I focused on the physical pain of damaged nipples as an example. There is no doubt that the psychological pain of exposing yourself to the part of your body that is triggering numerous times a day will also cause trauma. Despite how it can feel in the world of infant feeding, if you struggle with how your body looks and feels, you are not alone, and your feelings are real, valid, and you are deserving of support.

You Had to Stop

While genuinely needing to stop breastfeeding for medical reasons is uncommon, it is not unheard of. There are a handful of medications that you can't take while breastfeeding (although, far fewer than the inserts in medication packaging would have you believe). Sometimes, there isn't a safe alternative medication to try either. While some people will choose to sacrifice their health in order to breastfeed, this should be an individual choice that is made with someone's doctor and family, and judging someone for making a choice to be pain free, or able to function, over giving their baby human milk is not okay.

Cancer treatment is another reason for needing to stop breastfeeding. While there are cases where it's possible to continue during or after treatment, these are not typical. There can be a lot of guilt and grief that comes up when breastfeeding has to stop in this way, not to mention pressure to wean the baby or little one off the breast as quickly as possible so that treatment can be started. This is often traumatic for both the parents and the child. In fact, a cancer diagnosis is an extreme example of having your choice to breastfeed taken away from you, on top of having to face an exhausting treatment regime that leaves you too unwell to care for your baby, not to mention worries about your future.

You Were Simply Done

We don't talk enough about genuine choice in the world of breastfeeding. It's typically assumed that if you have the information and support that you need to breastfeed, then you'll do it. To admit that actually, you just don't enjoy breastfeeding, you feel trapped, low in mood, or like your body doesn't belong to you anymore, can be quite a taboo. It saddens me that we work so hard for women's rights, and advocate so strongly for our sisters to have access to genuine choices in life, but when it comes to breastfeeding, that choice is usually taken away from us. The rare times when it isn't, we're judged for choosing to stop. Frustratingly, this judgement only plays into the "breast is best vs. fed is best" narrative that makes lactation support appear to be exclusive and focused on "breastmilk at all costs." A narrative that makes people reluctant to seek support when they do need it.

You are your own person. You know what is happening inside your body and your mind far better than any number of studies, books, or professionals can ever understand. Breastfeeding in our modern world is a complex issue, fuelled by society's sexualisation of the female body, capitalism's need to sell formula as well as get parents back in to paid work, and a complete lack of meaningful and helpful support for mothers. Maybe you can't quite put your finger on why you stopped breastfeeding, but I'm willing to guess that, in addition to the factors mentioned above, at least one of the following was at play:

- You felt trapped or isolated.
- You were anxious about other people's opinions.
- You had a feeling of being touched too much, sometimes described as a skin crawling sensation around feeds.
- You were exhausted.
- You felt as though you had lost your identity.
- You were struggling to look after yourself physically or mentally.

- You experienced body dysphoria.
- You just felt an indescribable sense of "I am *done*."

Does choosing to stop for these sorts of reasons mean you didn't try hard enough to breastfeed? Absolutely not (and success should not be about effort, anyway)! You may have battled internally with yourself for some time about whether you should stop or not, or maybe you were able to advocate for yourself without too much internal conflict. That particular skill is something we should celebrate more.

Processing Your Grief in a World That Assumes You Didn't Try Hard Enough

One of the ironic side effects of a world that has normalised formula is that many people who successfully breastfeed will assume that if you're not breastfeeding, you didn't try hard enough. This tends to happen when someone has had what we might call "normal" problems establishing breastfeeding, such as a shallow latch needing some adjusting, or giving some top ups in the first few weeks. It's genuinely difficult to push through these issues, and it's understandable to think that people who don't breastfeed just didn't look for the right support or answers, especially if you know you had to work hard to breastfeed too.

The trouble is that misinformation is so common, that when there is a physiological or more complex reason for not breastfeeding, people might not even consider that's what happened to you. The issue then is, how do you begin to heal when, at every turn, you meet someone who tells you that they struggled too but worked hard and overcame the challenges? Or who writes a lengthy social media comment telling you that you just needed to try harder? I hope that Part Two of this book will offer you some support as you work through your feelings. For now, I see you and I believe you completely.

PART TWO:
RECOVERY

CHAPTER 8

Beginning to Heal

It is never too soon to begin the work of recovering from your breastfeeding grief or trauma. If you broke your arm, you wouldn't wait a few weeks before getting it treated. Our feelings are no different.

This part of the book will take you through several exercises you can do yourself to help your grieving and processing experience. You do not need to work through it in order, and you do not need to complete all or even most of them. They are here for you to take or leave as feels right for you.

Before you begin, I want to remind you that there is nothing wrong with you, or your feelings. The experience of loss you are dealing with, however it's coming up, is expected. Our society suffers from a significant lack of good support for dealing with grief in general, and especially so when it comes to infant feeding. You might even be surprised at how little support there seems to be out there about coping with loss in general. I would imagine you know how to apply basic first aid to a stranger in the street through training, but it's unlikely you've been taught how to apply emotional first aid for yourself or others when grieving or processing a difficult experience. This seems bizarre when we think about how broad grief is, and, therefore, how *common* it is. Far more people deal with grief every year than need to use CPR. This speaks volumes about how we live in a society that does a good job of looking after physical emergencies but is alarmingly clueless about emotional emergencies –something all humans will experience. With this in mind, try to approach the following chapters with an open mind. The techniques and thoughts I'm going to discuss might feel unfamiliar, therefore pointless. Take your time and be open to this evidence-based approach that is sadly not often discussed in everyday life.

Some Thoughts on Grief and Healing

We have been taught to grieve alone, and to experience difficult feelings alone. Do any of these statements sound familiar to you?

"Time heals all wounds."

"When you laugh, the whole world laughs with you.
  When you cry, you cry alone."

"Stop making a fuss."

"If you're going to cry like that, please go to your room."

"You need space."

"Just give things some time."

You have likely heard at least some of these from your childhood. Unfortunately, being taught that you need to be somehow polite and tidy in your feelings is unhelpful, and only encourages you to bottle up your feelings. Equally, being taught to simply wait for "time to heal all wounds" is unrealistic. If you had a headache that was stopping you from functioning, would you simply wait for it to pass? Most people will find some pain relief to support them to reach a point of functioning again. Difficult feelings are no different. You could sit and wait for them to pass, alone, unable to really live your life as you want to. Or you could take some steps to support yourself in your distress. In fact, a 2016 study concluded that using active coping skills is the most effective way of dealing with difficult feelings (Dijkstra & Homan, 2016). This may be because actively taking charge of your feelings gives humans a sense of control, something that is strongly associated with positive wellbeing. Some ways of being active in your processing are explored in more detail in the following chapters. For now, though, here are some quick tips:

- Write down your feelings in a journal, or in a letter to your baby. You could burn or tear up this letter or page once you're done with it or keep it if you think it might help to reread it later.

- Allow your feelings to be there. If you need to cry, cry. Sometimes you might feel a need to cry but be unable to fully access the depth of feelings needed to allow the tears to fall. Listening to music or watching a sad film can often help to open the floodgates. Remember that crying is cathartic. People typically feel better a little while after a good cry. If you're angry, express your anger. Push against a wall with your palms, putting your entire weight into trying to move the wall, go for a walk, or simply shake your body and stomp your feet until the feeling passes.

- Figure out a plan for if you want to breastfeed another baby. Problem solving in this way can be healing. What went wrong this time, and what might have led to a different outcome? Some people even decide to train to become a peer supporter at their local breastfeeding group or for a national helpline.

- Reframing. This is where you take a negative thought and change it to a positive or neutral one. "I failed my baby" becomes "My baby is thriving under my love and care."

- Connect with your baby in new ways. Meditation can be wonderful for feeling connected with your baby. There's one below that you might want to try. Also think about co-bathing, babywearing, baby massage, and simply playing with your little one now you aren't spending so much time focusing on getting feeding sorted.

A Meditation for Connection

This meditation is done while you are holding your baby.

1. Take a moment to relax and settle into a comfortable position.

2. Close your eyes and draw your attention to your baby. Notice their weight and warmth against your body. Listen to their breathing, notice their scent, and anything else that draws your attention, such as if they're holding your hand.

3. When you're ready, imagine a golden light is connecting your heart and your baby's heart. As you breathe in, the light flows from your baby to you, and as you breathe out, it flows back from you to the baby.

4. The longer you focus on this light, the more it fills you and the baby, spreading from your hearts to the rest of your bodies, and eventually creating a bubble around the two of you.

5. Stay with this moment for as long as you would like to. When you're ready, slowly bring your attention back to the room you're in and open your eyes.

6. You can do this meditation as often as you would like to.

CHAPTER NINE

Reframing Your Experience

What is Reframing?

Reframing is a term often used in therapy to describe the way we can look at something from a different angle. This change in perspective can help us to feel better about a situation, simply by considering that what happened may not be our fault. I believe that reframing is an essential part of dealing with breastfeeding grief and trauma. I feel it works so well because, if you didn't meet your breastfeeding goal, it really isn't your fault. Whether you had lack of support, lack of understanding, or you suffered from the effects of breast is best/fed is best, I completely believe you are not to blame.

Reframing Failure

I have lost count of how many times someone has told me they failed to breastfeed, despite providing their own milk to their baby for a period of time. Providing your baby with any of your milk is a success. You produced breastmilk and your baby took that milk. Your baby was absolutely breastfed, as far as I'm concerned.

I know that there is a *lot* more to this than such a personal definition of "breastfed," though. If it was truly that simple, this book wouldn't need to exist. The point of reframing isn't to downplay your feelings but to see things from a slightly different angle.

I'm not here to lie to you, or to sell you a fantasy. You didn't meet your goals. Breastfeeding wasn't how you imagined or wanted it to be. That is such a lot to carry, and your feelings are real. However, it is also true that if your baby latched, you breastfed them. If you expressed your milk and fed it to your baby in a syringe, tube, bottle, or cup, you gave them your breastmilk. You succeeded at those things.

Instead of saying "I couldn't breastfeed" or "I failed to breast-feed," you might want to try some of the reframes listed below. Notice if the shift in language feels lighter, even slightly. That lightness is what you're looking for to tell you that you're on the right track.

- I breastfed for X days.
- I successfully gave my baby my own milk for X days.
- My baby got my milk.
- I produced enough for the baby to have some human milk every day for X duration.
- It hurt, and I still did it.
- I'm proud we managed to feed for X amount of time.

More General Examples of Reframing

Let's run through some examples of reframing. If you find these helpful, please consider using them as affirmations. If not, then you can make your own. Affirmations can work well written on Post-it notes, which are then placed on mirrors or other places you might see them. You can also just repeat them to yourself each morning or while you're making breakfast, for example.

"I should have seen an IBCLC, but I didn't".

Reframes:

- IBCLCs should be easier to access.
- If society supported infant feeding, an IBCLC would have been more accessible.
- No one taught me what an IBCLC could do.

Take comfort:

It's easy to tell yourself that you should have seen an IBCLC, a tongue tie practitioner, or any other number of infant experts. However, if you didn't, that will have been because of a few reasons, none of which are your fault. For example:

- The cost was too high.
- There was no one available in your area.
- You hadn't been told exactly what an IBCLC is.
- You had been led to believe that midwives are the experts on infant feeding.
- You were told an infant feeding expert would judge you for using formula.

Ask yourself; if you needed to see a chiropractor, would you have to dig around to find out what one is, where and when you can see one, and why they might be helpful? You see the GP for a bad back and the doctor tells you that a chiropractor or osteopath is worth seeing. They may even give you a leaflet about this private practice professional who isn't funded by the NHS. But when it comes to lactation, you are met with raised eyebrows, gatekeeping, minimising, and lack of access if you want to see a private professional. None of this is your fault. You are not to blame for not seeing the right person at the right time. You were dealing with more than enough as a new, exhausted, and worried parent, without needing to research and fund appropriate breastfeeding support because your country doesn't take it seriously.

"I was letting my baby starve."

Reframes:

- The professionals around me didn't notice my baby was struggling.
- I knew something was wrong and I asked for help (but I was dismissed/wrongly reassured).
- My baby is happy and healthy now because of the actions I took when I saw a problem.

Take comfort:

No good parent lets their baby starve. You take context cues from the people around you who are portrayed as wiser. Often, this is a medical professional when it comes to infant feeding and care. If someone had said to you, "Okay, your baby is not gaining enough weight, and this is worrying because of the risk of XYX," you would have followed whatever instructions you were given because it is natural to trust the professionals on your team. You *should* be able to trust them.

This issue is even more complex, because the chances are, you were told how important breastfeeding is and how easy it is to be persuaded to use formula. This can leave you in an impossible situation where you believe giving formula will ruin your chances of breastfeeding successfully **and** the professionals are telling you that things are okay or that they just want to "keep a little bit of a closer eye on you–nothing to worry about." All of these messages, combined with exhaustion and postnatal hormones, are excellent at drowning out that little voice that might have been whispering to you that something wasn't quite right. We're taught to ignore our intuition from early on, especially as women and female-presenting individuals. Why would you trust it with a new baby when you've been told that everything you do is too much or not enough, and that you are always wrong?

> *"I should never have given my baby formula."*

Reframes:

- Formula is growing my baby.
- I love the eye contact we can make during bottle feeds.
- I made the right decision with the information I had at the time.

Take comfort:

Why did you give your baby formula? Was it because you had a niggling thought that something was wrong? Was it because you were exhausted and overwhelmed? Because you needed to get a break? You had to go back to work? You were told to?

All of those scenarios tell me one thing; you did what you needed to do at that moment. Whether for your health or the health of your baby. What an amazingly intuitive thing to do, to see that something needs to happen and *do it*, even when you don't want to. That's a good definition of selflessness right there.

"I wish I didn't listen to the doctor who said I needed to stop."

Reframes:

- I wish our country had better lactation training for doctors.

- I trusted a professional– they should have all the information and my best interests at heart.

- I made my decision to stop breastfeeding based on the information I was given by a trusted professional.

Take comfort:

We grow up being taught that doctors are the experts, and that we must listen to them. We are also warned about medication passing into breastmilk, and while this is rarely a significant concern, you would hope and expect that the person issuing the medication would be confident as to whether or not it can be safely prescribed. You listened to your doctor because you were placed in a position where you were led to believe that you had to weigh up the risks to your baby and your health and make a decision that increased the risks for one of you. Probably in a 10-minute consultation, while the doctor told you that formula is fine, and that breastfeeding doesn't work for everyone. How could you possibly have made a different choice in that moment?

> *"I'm such a failure."*

Reframes:

- My baby loves me.
- I nurture my baby with hugs and closeness.
- I am working hard for my baby.
- I am a good parent.

Take comfort:

I firmly believe that you did not fail. You were given misinformation, no information, you were unsupported, and you brought a baby into a world that wants you to formula feed. You were failed by the systems and people around you, but *you* did not fail.

Reframing – Thought by Thought.

This is an exercise you can do in writing, or just while sitting quietly. It can also work well if you're stuck in a loop of intrusive thoughts about your breastfeeding journey, or if every reframe you come up with is met with a retort from your brain. I'll use an example below, but I hope you will be able to apply it to your own situation and individual thoughts.

> *"I'm such a failure; I couldn't even breastfeed my own baby!"*

Reframe: "I successfully breastfed for 3 weeks."

*"Three weeks is **nothing**. I wanted to do it for 2 years."*

Reframe: "I worked so hard at breastfeeding and overcame many obstacles."

"Not enough! I should have gotten more support."

Reframe: "Support needs to be easier to access."

"I should have tried harder."

Reframe: "I'm so angry that the government doesn't fund the lactation support that would have given me more options than simply trying."

In this example, we've moved from feeling ashamed and guilty about our perceived failure, to angry at the government. Anger can be a positive emotion if we channel it correctly. You can write to your MP, make a donation to a breastfeeding charity, stomp your feet, punch a pillow, scribble on paper–whatever feels like a safe way to move that anger through your body.

CHAPTER TEN

Reconnection

Breastfeeding necessitates a lot of connection. Every time you lift your top to feed your baby, you are facilitating a degree of skin-to-skin contact with them, even if it's only cheek to chest. Your baby will typically be held by you, as you are the only one able to settle them with your breast. Once you stop breastfeeding, it is common to automatically lose a certain amount of that physical contact, and for many parents, this can contribute to feeling a loss of closeness with their baby. Fortunately, there are many more ways to bond and be close with your baby than breastfeeding. In fact, if you have spent a lot of time pumping or in pain, you might even find that, in some ways, you now have *more* time to enjoy your little one. You might need to be a little more deliberate in how you seek and provide close connection, but that doesn't need to be a barrier.

There is, of course, another part to reconnection, and that is reconnection with your body. Or, in many cases, connection for the first time with your body. If breastfeeding has been difficult, you may end up feeling that you can't trust your body; this is on top of dealing with the common experience of your body physically looking different after pregnancy compared to before. This distrust can lead to a range of difficulties from a simple disconnect right up to self-hatred. While this book can't cure the lack of trust and connection you might be feeling towards your body, there are a couple of gentle exercises in this chapter that you might feel able to explore.

Important Note

Some of these techniques might be too much for you if you are holding onto a lot of trauma around breastfeeding, or if you stopped recently. It's okay to adapt the suggestions below to involve less skin to skin, or to be less intense. It's also totally okay to do only some, or even none, of these activities.

Skin to Skin Feeding

When we bottle feed, we tend to do it fully clothed. This means you are immediately given multiple opportunities each day to experience skin to skin contact with your baby. We understand that skin to skin contact is important in bonding and connection, in part due to the release of the hormone oxytocin. Obviously, it is unrealistic to feed your baby topless for every single feed, but it can be a lovely ritual to build into a morning or evening routine. You may even be able to snuggle your baby upright, close to your breast, to make the feed feel even closer to the breastfeeding experience.

Co-Bathing/Showering

Co-bathing is often recommended to improve breastfeeding problems, but it can also be incredibly powerful to rebuild any sense of lost connection you might be feeling. While you could simply hop in the bath and lay the baby on your tummy or hold them skin to skin under a gentle shower, you might want to move through a ritual called "rebirthing." If you do, here's how:

- Try to recreate anything you wanted or enjoyed about your birthing space. Music, low lighting, affirmations, etc.

- Fill your bath with comfortably warm water; it needs to be deep enough for you and the baby. You might even want to use a birthing pool if you have access to one.

- Some people like to put some defrosted breastmilk in the bath, or some rose petals or lavender flowers. These can remind us to relax and soak up feelings of love and peace. The breastmilk acts as a fantastic moisturiser and may symbolically feel important as you thank your body for the milk it produced.

- When ready, have your partner place your baby in the water between your legs (head exposed). You can then reach down to take the baby, lifting them onto your body as you may have done, or wanted to do after they were born,

- Stay with your baby in the water, relaxing and enjoying each other as you reconnect. Move through the motions a new mother often makes in the minutes after her baby is born. She will typically explore her infant's body, one place at a time, sniffing his head, tracing her fingers over his body, holding his feet and hands, talking gently to him, etc.

- Your baby might try to latch to your breast. If you don't want this to happen, you could hold them a little lower, on your tummy rather than your chest. You could also end the ritual if the baby begins to root for the breast. Alternatively, you might want to use this moment as your last breastfeed, allowing any sadness to wash over you as you say goodbye to this part of your parenting journey. Your partner could take photos for you, if that felt right.

Massage

In its most simple form, baby massage is skin to skin touch, something we have already discussed above as becoming less available once breastfeeding ends. Massage is also more than that, though. Baby massage is now commonly used with parents who are experiencing depression or difficulties connecting with their infants for a multitude of reasons. It was deemed so helpful and important when I worked for our local Sure Start Children's Centres that it was made a "universal offering," meaning anyone could book in and attend instead of the usual criteria for support needing to be met. Baby massage teaches parents to actively support their baby with issues like tummy pain, to encourage the across midline movements needed to prepare the baby for crawling, releases oxytocin in the parent and baby, and promotes eye contact (Gürol & Polat, 2012; Mrljak et al., 2022). It also teaches you recognise and respond to "ready" and "I've had enough" cues that babies will demonstrate when we tune in to them. Even if you already know all of these things, baby massage helps parents to feel confident and empowered in the care of their little one (Khuzaiyah et al., 2022).

Baby massage should always be taught by a trained practitioner, and there are times you should not massage your baby (i.e. if they are unwell or have had vaccinations recently). There are, however, some simple and generally safe massage strokes you can use at any time. Below, I'll talk you through a gentle hand massage you can do with your baby:

- Hold the baby's hand in yours and use your thumb to make small circles around their palm. Your movements should be gentle but firm, and your thumb should remain in contact with your baby's hand at all times. You can use a drop of coconut or sunflower oil, or no oil at all.

- Next, you can gently squeeze and roll each of your baby's fingers between your thumb and forefinger as you move from the base of each finger to the tip. The movement is a kind of rhythmic wiggle or rocking as you work up each finger.

- You can repeat these movements with your baby's feet, applying slightly more pressure than with the hands, but still taking care to be gentle.

- Always stop if your baby disengages with you or seems uncomfortable in any way.

Babywearing

Carrying your baby in sling, wrap, or carrier, has some wonderful benefits for you and your little one. These include less infant crying and a stronger feeling of connection between the two of you (Grisham et al., 2023). When mothers stop breastfeeding, they often describe feeling as though they're not sure how to comfort their little one without the breast, and babywearing can be a fantastic way to do that. You're close to each other, your baby will often sleep or simply enjoy being with you as you move through your day, **and** you have your hands free to do other things.

There are some safety guidelines for babywearing, so please do bear these in mind.

- The sling should be tight enough so the baby can't slip down.

- Your baby's face should be in view at all times.

- Their head should be close enough for you to kiss.

- Their chin should be lifted, away from their chest.

- Your baby should be well supported along their back.

I also recommend talking to someone trained in babywearing (such as a sling consultant or peer supporter) before you use a sling for the first time.

Reading and Playing

Often when I work with mums who have been trying to make breastfeeding work, they've become so consumed with pumping, latching, or readjusting that they haven't had the headspace to simply sit and be with their baby. They commonly tell me "I feel like I'm missing out on this time." So, if you've reached the point of no longer breastfeeding, you might now want to spend time just enjoying your little one. Even newborns love the sound of your voice as you read to them, especially if they're snuggled up against your chest.

When it comes to playing, *you* are the best toy your baby has. They will be fascinated by everything you do, and perhaps you haven't had much opportunity to notice or enjoy that if breastfeeding has been hard. If you sit your baby facing you on your raised knees and pull faces at them, they will try to copy you, smile, and even laugh as they get older. Songs, finger rhymes, and peekaboo are all classic activities that can help you to feel close and happy with your baby as you work to recover from the pain and hurt you've been through.

Reconnecting with Your Body

If you feel like you've failed to breastfeed, this may extend to a feeling that your body has failed. As we live in a world where women are given a message of being "too much" or "not enough" from early in life, this feeling of disconnection or even hatred of your own body when breastfeeding doesn't work out is not surprising to me at all. If we add in a difficult pregnancy, IFV, and/

or birth experience, then that disappointment or anger may be intensified. While healing your relationship with your body may be a long-term project, there are some small things you might like to try to begin to feel grounded and connected just a little bit more. These suggestions are simple and not especially intense, but as always, listen to your instincts and stop/skip if you need to.

Feel Your Feet

This is a simple grounding technique that can gently bring you back into your body. Simply feel your bare feet on the ground. It can feel especially good on grass or a beach, but any floor will do. Take a deep breath as you plant your feet firmly on the ground. Notice if they're touching something warm, cool, smooth, soft, prickly, etc.

If you want to extend this, you could imagine roots coming out of the soles of your feet and shooting down into the earth. Many people like to "see" these roots reach the centre of the Earth and connect into a ball of light there. They will then imagine light from this source entering their roots and pouring back up to fill their entire body.

Joyful Movement

Movement simply for the joy of it can come in so many forms, it would be impossible to list them all. As a silly example, though, I absolutely love to slide around corners in my house, thanks to the combination of laminate flooring and socks. To the horror of my children, sometimes I'll give an enthusiastic "Katchow!" as I skid into the room. There is absolutely no reason for this silliness, other than it bringing me a moment of childlike joy to my neurodivergent brain. I'm sharing this because it's such a small thing, but it brings a little bit of joy into the everyday. You don't need to go for a hike, do an hour of yoga, or go to a dance class to move with joy. It can be as simple as being grateful for a moment that your body does what it does. We're just looking to lift some of the negativity or disconnection you might be feeling here, to notice that your body can be used for fun, and that it does that well.

If neither of these ideas do it for you, here's an incomplete list of ways you might be able to reconnect with your body:

- Stretching
- Yoga
- Exercise
- Sex
- Dance
- Meditation
- Art
- Hugs
- Massage

Reconnecting with Your Values

Breastfeeding may have been a big part of your identity as a parent. You may have imagined a beautiful experience that solved all of your baby's problems. You may have loved breastfeeding, and not know who you are now that it's ended. Mums often tell me they feel lost when breastfeeding ends, and they don't know how to parent without it. This can intertwine with grief and shame, as well as contribute to the feelings of failure already showing up. However, whether you are breastfeeding or not, you have values and beliefs that are important to you, and you don't need to breastfeed to keep yourself aligned with those ideas. Below is an exercise many of the parents I work with find helpful. See if it resonates for you:

What Was it About Breastfeeding That Was Important to Me as a Parent and as a Person?

For example:

- ☐ It provided excellent nutrition.
- ☐ It helped to stop my little one crying.
- ☐ It was a reason to stay close by my baby.
- ☐ It gave me time to relax with my baby.
- ☐ It protected against illness.
- ☐ I felt deeply connected to my baby during breastfeeding.

What Parenting Values Show Up in My List?

- ☐ Health and nutrition
- ☐ Being a responsive parent
- ☐ Feeling connected to my child

How Can I Meet Those Values Without Breastfeeding?

Health and Nutrition:

☐ I can feed my baby according to their hunger and satiety cues. This can teach a healthy attitude towards food, which has a positive impact on health later in life.

☐ I can provide nutritious solids when the time is right.

☐ I can introduce solids responsively, trusting my baby to take what they need, when they need it.

Being a Responsive Parent:

☐ I can pace bottle feeds.

☐ I can babywear, cuddle, or rock my baby when they cry.

☐ I can allow my baby to stop feeding or eating when they tell me they're full.

☐ I know what my baby likes or doesn't like, and I respond accordingly.

Feeling Connected to My Child:

☐ Babywearing

☐ Baby massage

☐ Co-bathing

☐ Responding to them when they cry, smile, babble, need a nappy change

☐ Feel baby cuddled into me

☐ Skin to skin

☐ Playtime

What Can I Do When Feelings of Guilt Come Up?

☐ Notice the feeling

Sometimes, we try to push through feelings or ignore them, but they'll keep coming back if we do that. When you're able to, pause, notice it, and name it ("I'm feeling shame because I'm bottle feeding").

Recognise That My Brain is Telling Me a Story

Our brains are tricky things. They're essentially trying to keep us safe, but they're not always good at it. You *want* to breastfeed, so your brain is telling you you're failing by not breastfeeding to try and make you start again. Even though you have acknowledged and understood that this isn't right or possible for your situation, it can be helpful to take a moment to acknowledge that your brain is trying to help you here. You might say, "Thank you, brain, for wanting to keep me safe." You could then bring some acknowledgement into the situation by saying, "You've told me this story about being a bad mum lots of times."

List All of the Ways I Am Meeting My Little One's Needs

Next, you bring your attention back to reality. "I am meeting my baby's needs by..." and list some of the values you identified above. If your brain returns to its story of you being a bad parent, thank it for trying to help you, and move on to the last step.

Go and Connect with My Baby

Try to do this mindfully. If your baby is sleeping, go and look at them. Notice as much as you can about them. If they're awake, you could do some baby massage, or play a game. Again, noticing everything you can. Their hair, the way they smell, the noises they make, how you know if they're enjoying your time together. Anytime your brain starts with its "bad mum" story, just bring your focus back to the baby.

CHAPTER ELEVEN

Feeling Proud

Pride is a strange thing in our world. Often, people feel it's something to be minimised for fear of vanity. However, feeling proud of yourself is an amazing power to have. If *you* feel proud of you, there's no need to have validation from other people. Of course, having others also express pride at your successes is a positive thing too, but it's empowering to not *need* that external support. Pride also leads to feelings of fulfilment and improved self-esteem.

Reasons to be Proud

When I was struggling to breastfeed my eldest, I had a sheet of paper a midwife had given me. It was a chart that consisted of the amount of time a baby was breastfed in days, weeks, and months, and the benefits that my baby had received as a result. So, I could look at this chart stuck to my fridge and see that 2 weeks of breastfeeding meant my baby's transition into the world had been eased by breastfeeding, and that his gut was protected because of my milk. It was helpful, but the problem was that I would skip ahead and see that if I breastfed him for a year, he'd be less likely to get sick when he started daycare. Then, I would feel anxious and guilty because I couldn't see myself feeding him beyond a month. So, this section isn't going to tell you the reasons to be proud based on how long you breastfed. There are many reasons for you to feel good, without minimum requirements.

Some examples of reasons to be proud (that aren't to do with the volume of human milk):

Being Willing to Try

If you had a hard time breastfeeding before, and you still gave it a go with your next baby, that's genuinely amazing. If your baby didn't latch on the first day and you just started hand expressing instead of reaching for formula, that shows your willingness to try. You didn't have to try; it would have been easier not to. But you didn't take that easier path, you gave it a go.

Asking for Help

We live in a world that seems to look down on asking for help. People often pride themselves on *not* reaching out for support, or for being hyper independent. It's also difficult to access lactation support if you need something more specialised. You can't just go to the doctor and get a referral to an IBCLC and a tongue-tie provider. You have to find these people, vet them yourself, and pay out of pocket (at least in the UK, if you take the private route). All of this has to be done while dealing with pain, recovering from birth, and running on next to no sleep. If you can't afford to access this level of support, you probably turned to social media, friends, acquaintances, and helplines, all of which require you to seek them out, articulate your issue, and figure out a plan. Honestly, this isn't easy to do on any level. Practically, it takes up time and headspace, and it's not something we're used to doing on a societal or psychological level.

Persevering Through Challenges

It often feels like you're being told to use formula at every turn. Whether it's top ups for slow weight gain (instead of pumping or donor milk) or giving a bottle so your nipples can have a break from the pain, formula is usually the solution offered for breast-feeding problems. Every time you said no to that bottle and chose a different path (more pumping, more pain), you showed strength in committing to do something that felt important to you. You stood up to people in a position of authority and you listened to your instincts. All of these things can be so hard to do in a paternalistic society. You pushed against the narrative, and you worked as hard as you could, for as long as felt right.

Advocating for Your Choices

Similar to the paragraph above, advocating for your choices is hard to do for a lot of people. We are taught from a young age to listen to doctors and other medical professionals. Sadly, when it comes to infant feeding, these people are usually not the experts, but it can feel frightening to make a different choice to their rec-ommendation. Standing up for your choices and wishes takes a lot of courage.

Strength in Admitting When Enough is Enough

We can get so caught up in the importance of advocating for your right to breastfeed that we might forget there is also a huge display of strength in deciding it's time to stop. When you want something so badly that you've put yourself through pain or a strict routine multiple times a day for weeks or months, to then hold your hands up and admit you're done can feel like a huge failure. It's not, though. It's seeing the bigger picture and being able to let go of one hope in order to pursue something bigger.

A Space for You to Share What You're Proud of

Please use the space below you share your own reasons to be proud of your feeding and parenting journey:

CHAPTER TWELVE

A Space for Debriefing

What is a Debrief?

Debrief is probably not quite the correct term to use to describe the process of making sense of your experience with someone qualified in counselling skills and/or lactation knowledge. Traditionally, debriefs are used to refer to the process of sharing information after a project or even a military operation. In a clinical sense, debriefing is a structured meeting between a group of professionals who get together to talk about a case and the learning to be gleaned from it.

A breastfeeding debrief is essentially a counselling session. Unlike traditional counselling, however, it tends to happen only once or twice. The person guiding you through the debrief doesn't need to be a therapist, nor do they need a particularly deep understanding of lactation. There is also no formal method that every practitioner uses. Essentially, we have come to the term debrief because "a safe space to tell your story and feel your feelings, while also getting some information about why things went wrong" isn't catchy.

In this chapter I will walk you through the steps I usually take parents through when they book a debrief with me. I encourage you to write down your answers to the questions posed, or to talk them through with someone you trust. Each section will also include an example to help with anything that's coming up blank for you.

What Happened?

Usually, people start with their birth experience and run through their experiences in chronological order. You don't need to do this, though. Perhaps one particular experience or moment in your breastfeeding journey jumps out to you as the most important or upsetting.

> *Things started to go wrong from the first feed. I wanted to do a breast crawl, but the midwives seemed to be impatient to get the baby to latch. Someone took my breast in one hand, my baby in the other, and sort of shoved us together. It hurt, but I didn't want to complain. After that, it got more and more painful with every feed, and by day 4, we were back in the hospital because the baby had jaundice. On day 5, he lost 11% of his birth weight, and I was told to top up. My nipples were ripped to shreds and I was exhausted so I decided to just stop breastfeeding.*

How Did it Feel?

Try to see beyond labelling your feelings. What does that sadness or anger feel like in your body? Where is it? Does it feel like a little spikey ball of black energy deep in your core, or is it an oozing, tar like feeling that spreads through your entire body? Is it hot? Cold? An ache?

> *I felt relief at first – it was like a lightness washed over me. But as my breasts began to get fuller, I started to feel tearful. It was like a heavy ache in my chest and throat, and I couldn't really explain it. I just felt a strong sense of hot, burning shame and sadness.*

What was the Outcome?

Did you continue to breastfeed, or stop? Was there any long-term impact on your mood or how you felt or feel as a parent?

> After I stopped breastfeeding, I felt low in mood and didn't want to hold or feed my baby. Everyone told me that it didn't matter and that he was healthy, but I still felt heavy. It took a few weeks for me to stop feeling sad every time I gave him a bottle, and now I'm anxious about trying to breastfeed next time.

What Would You Change if You Could?

Would you have accessed different support? Would you have stopped sooner? Carried on for longer?

> I wish I had advocated more strongly to be left alone after the birth. I also think I could have asked for more support with my sore nipples, and if I'd understood that the pain wasn't normal, I might have been able to get help and breastfeed for longer. I also think I could have asked to express and give that to my baby when we were in for jaundice, instead of just accepting the formula.

What Did You Need Access to That You Couldn't Get?

Hopefully, by this point in the book, you have a clear idea of this. Did you need an IBCLC, a support group, a book, or a tongue tie assessment? More or different help from your family?

> More knowledge of my options, some information in pregnancy, and professionals who knew how to help me succeed instead of seeing me as a box to tick.

What Would You Say to the People Who Let You Down if You Could?

This question can cause people to recoil and hold back. We are so-cialised to avoid expressing harsh words or to share the true depth of our pain. This is a safe space, though. Perhaps you could write a letter to the person you feel failed you the most, and then burn it when you're ready. Really let your feelings go here; any words, however shocking they might seem, are welcome.

> *I thought there was something wrong with me, but what was wrong was the "support" I got. I am so angry that I was let down in this way, and that, at no point, did someone try to help me succeed at breastfeeding. I will never get that time back, and all I remember of it is feeling stressed and in pain. You ruined the first days and weeks of motherhood for me.*

What Did You Learn (How Has This Experience Helped You to Grow as a Person)?

When you've been stuck in your feelings of failure, it can be hard to see any positives to your journey. However, there will almost always be something. Did you learn that you were more resilient than you realised? That your maternal instinct is strong? That pa-tience is an important life skill?

> *I have learned that I am the only person who can stand up for my rights and the rights of my baby. And I have learned that I **can** do that. I feel much stronger as a woman and as a mother because of my anger.*

What Do You Love About Being a Parent?

Breastfeeding doesn't define you as a parent. What else do you enjoy about this incredible experience?

> *I love how when he wakes up in the morning and sees me, he has this huge smile on his face. Like I'm the best person in the world. I also love just being with him. Going to groups, or playing together at home. He makes me happy even on the hardest days.*

How Does Your Baby Show You That They Love You?

Parents often feel that breastfeeding was the only thing their baby loved about them. As someone who has spent my entire career watching parents and babies interact, regardless of feeding method, I have seen countless times the way a baby will search the room for Mum, or snuggle into their chest for a nap after refusing to do this for anyone else. If you can't think of anything, perhaps a loved one can share what they've noticed about your baby's reaction to you?

> *He smiles when he sees me, looks for me if he can't see me, and he is comforted when I hold him. He cries for most people except me.*

The Three Step Rewind Technique

The Three Step Rewind is a short course of non-invasive PTSD ther-apy that's often used in birth trauma. Recently, birth and lactation professionals have begun to use it for breastfeeding grief and trauma as well. The process consists of 3 steps:

1. Sharing your experience

2. Visualisation while in a deeply relaxed state

3. Picturing coping going forward and reacting differently to before

The Three Step Rewind should be done with a professional trained in the approach. It's well worth considering, as it appears to be safe and effective with most people saying that their heavy and difficult feelings ease by the end of the treatment, and that this relief lasts afterwards.

CHAPTER THIRTEEN

Next Time

While it's common (and completely valid) to decide not to breast-feed next time if you had problems before, lots of women *do* want to try again. If this is you, then the following chapter will guide you through a plan for success.

1. Before Your Baby is Born

Before your baby is even born is an important time for you to plan how you're going to succeed at breastfeeding. If a lack of information was problematic for you last time, then now is the time to fill in those gaps in your knowledge. Attend a preparing to breastfeed class, go to your local peer support group, or buy some up-to date-books, such as *The Positive Breastfeeding Book* by Amy Brown or *Breastfeeding Doesn't Need to Suck* by Kathleen Kendall-Tackett. If you're still having some difficult feelings come up from your last experience, this is also a good time to have a one-to-one debrief with an IBCLC or breastfeeding counsellor, even if you've had one before. You might even want to consider some counselling sessions or three-step rewind.

While you're preparing with your education, also think about the day-to-day experience of life with a newborn. What did you struggle with last time? Was it lack of sleep? Feeling isolated? The house being messy? Not having time to prepare the food that makes you feel your best? Once you pinpoint the challenges, you can plan for them to be easier this time through, calling in extra support. Whether that's a friend or family member, or you hire a doula, a cleaner, or find some high-quality ready meals to be delivered. Also, have the details of your local breastfeeding support services to hand, whether voluntary or private. I often get text messages on the day of birth with second-time parents keen to book me in immediately.

Consider hand expressing your colostrum in the last weeks of pregnancy (if your provider gives you the go ahead). While it's true that some parents are unable to see any milk when they do this, many do get a nice amount of colostrum that they can freeze in case it's needed, and even if you don't, you're still learning a valuable skill that could be useful after your baby is born.

Finally, it can be helpful to talk to your friends, family, and support network about your plans to breastfeed, and let them know how they can support you to achieve your goals. Perhaps they can help with household chores or childcare, for example, or be available to take you to a breastfeeding support group.

2. The Time Between Birth and Your Milk Coming In

It almost goes without saying that having skin to skin contact with your baby as soon as possible is the first, and usually the easiest, thing you can do to help breastfeeding get off to a good start. This is particularly the case if your baby is allowed to wriggle up to find the breast themselves over an hour or so. If skin to skin isn't possible, having two little blankets or even reusable breast pads that you switch between you and your baby every day if they're in NICU can be supportive for bonding and oxytocin; your baby will get to smell you, and you'll get to smell them. Skin to skin and the breast crawl (that wriggling up the breast) can happen weeks after birth, so you can recreate this later if need be.

Another thing you can do in those first days is hand express after a few feeds each day. This doesn't need to be a lot, or even after every feed. What you're aiming for here is a little extra breast stimulation, and perhaps a few drops of milk to pop in the fridge, so that if your baby is struggling with their latch, you have still primed your breasts well and have some supplements of your own milk ready to feed your baby when, or if, they are needed.

3. Are Things Going Well?

After a traumatic or simply a difficult experience with breast-feeding, it's common for parents to worry about whether things are going down the same path next time. Let's go over a sort of lactation triage here, to help you figure out if you need more help or not.

- **Is Breastfeeding Comfortable for You?**

By this, I mean, are you in pain? Because you absolutely should not be in pain, beyond a bit of nipple stretching at the start of feeds in the first couple of days. Painful breastfeeding is nearly always caused by a shallow latch, which is common as the baby and parent learn how to fit together. Other signs that this might be a problem for you and your baby include cracked, bleeding nipples, or a nipple that comes out of the baby's mouth shaped like a new lipstick, blanched, or with a line across the top.

- **Is Your Baby Able to Go to the Breast and Actively Feed?**

Sometimes newborns are tricky. My youngest was one of these. He absolutely would not feed. To start with this looked like him opening his mouth and then just staying still, staring up at me with confusion on his face. Eventually, it morphed into him arch-ing his back and screaming when I tried to latch him. This could be your experience too, and while there are a host of possible reasons for it, a good place to start is a rebirthing ritual, which is discussed in Chapter Ten. If that doesn't help, then a careful oral assessment with a practitioner who understands the importance of being gentle with these orally-adverse babies will hopefully start to give you an idea as to whether a tongue tie or other oral issues causing the inability to feed.

- **Are You Seeing Wet Nappies?**

If it's going in, it's got to come out again! We like to see one wet nappy in the first 24 hours of life, 2 on day 2, etc., until your milk comes in and, at that point, we would hope that your baby will produce around 6 heavy wet nappies a day (or that the nappy will be noticeably wet at most changes). The urine should be pale in colour and not smell too strong. If that isn't the case, you need to talk to your care provider to have your baby assessed for dehydration.

- **Are You Seeing Dirty Nappies?**

One of the hardest myths to shift about breastfed babies is the one that says they don't need to open their bowels every day. They absolutely *should* be giving you dirty nappies every single day in the first 6 weeks. This is because the composition of human milk during this time is high in an ingredient called whey, which is fast to digest. Things that digest quickly are going to be seen at the other end of the digestive system quickly. After 6 weeks, babies might start to poo less often since, at this point, breast-milk has higher levels of another ingredient called casein, which is slower to digest. You might notice your 6-week-old only opens their bowels every other day or sometimes less often. As long as the other guidelines in this chapter are as expected, and your baby is happy, then after 6 weeks this reduction in dirty nappies is not usually a concern on its own.

- **Is Day 5 Weight Loss Less Than 7-10%?**

This is often seen as the true measure of how things are going. A weight loss of between 7% and 10% on day 5 after birth can tell us that the baby is struggling to take on enough milk. Most often this will be due to a shallow latch or a sleepy baby. Most UK NHS trusts won't worry until the baby has lost around 10% of their weight, but depending on the bigger picture, it's worth paying attention to a loss of 7-8%, as this might suggest you need some extra help now before things get harder to manage (Noel-Weiss et al., 2008).

- **Is The Baby Back to Birth Weight Around Week 2?**

There is some flexibility here, depending on weight loss at day 5. In some cases, it can take 3 weeks to return to birth weight, but we can usually say a baby who has gotten back to this weight by week 2 is taking on the milk they need, and milk supply is working as it should be (Noel-Weiss et al., 2008).

- **Is Your Baby Often (Not Always) Content and Relaxed After Feeding?**

A baby who falls off the breast in a contented sleep after a relaxed feed is a lovely sign that they're full up with milk. You might notice their fists are unclenched too. Sometimes they'll come away from the breast awake and just be content to look around, often up at you. It's normal for them to cue to feed again after a few minutes; babies often view breastfeeding as a three-course dinner, with little breaks in between, like at a restaurant. What you shouldn't be seeing often is a baby that goes to the breast unsettled, and then comes away from the breast even more annoyed.

This can absolutely happen as part of cluster feeding, or randomly here and there in the day, but you should see that more feeds end with a happy baby than with a grumpy one.

- **Is the Baby Feeding at Least 8 Times Per 24 Hours?**

Sleepy babies can be tricky to feed. They will often sleep through hunger cues, and if they're struggling with feeding, this can sometimes get worse as they try to retain energy. One big red flag for me is a baby struggling to gain weight that is sleeping through the night at just a few weeks of age. If they're gaining weight well and feeding often the rest of the time, this is okay, but with slow weight gain or a baby that's generally hard to feed, it becomes a worry.

Your baby will most likely want to feed between 8 and 12 times a day, although up to 16 times a day can be okay too (if everything else is on track) (Kent et al., 2006).

If your answer to all of the above questions is "yes," then that's amazing! It's likely that your baby is doing okay, and whatever you're experiencing is normal. However, if you have *any* doubts at all, please do seek some more support from a breastfeeding supporter, such as a Breastfeeding Counsellor or a support worker.

4. Seeking Extra Support

Of course, if things are not going well, or even if you feel like you just need a bit of reassurance, it's a great idea to check in with someone who is specifically trained to help with breastfeeding. These people tend to fall into one of five categories:

- Peer supporter
- Breastfeeding Counsellor

- Breastfeeding Helplines
- Infant feeding Support worker
- IBCLC or equivalent

All of these people are trained in breastfeeding support and can help you with feeding challenges and worries, and all of them will be able to signpost you to another type of support if they can't help you. There is absolutely no shame in seeking support for problems. In fact, given everything we have discussed in these pages, I hope you can see it is important to seek the *right* support to help you overcome challenges.

CHAPTER FOURTEEN

If You Need More Support, And Final Thoughts

While I wish that a book could heal everyone's grief and trauma around breastfeeding, that just isn't possible. So, this chapter will go through some further options you have if you need more help.

Depression and "Failed" Breastfeeding

When someone wants to breastfeed but doesn't meet their goal, they are at a significantly increased risk of postnatal depression (Brown et al., 2016). This is especially true for people who experienced pain during breastfeeding. We've already looked a lot at mental health and lactation in this book; it makes sense that you might feel depressed if you didn't meet your breastfeeding goal, not only from a psychological perspective, but from a physical one as well. There is a theory that when we stop producing milk suddenly, the primal part of our brains believes that our baby is no longer with us. Alongside the drastic shift in hormones that ending lactation quickly causes, it's not surprising that this results in low mood or even postnatal depression. Essentially, if you are feeling depressed after ending breastfeeding, you are far from alone. Many other parents experience the same feelings. While knowing this won't cure your depression, I do think we should be normalising these feelings to remove the added shame and stigma that tends to make depressive disorders worse for longer.

National Helplines

A first step to healing can often be talking about what happened. While you wrote down your thoughts and feelings in the debrief section of this book, actually saying the words can be more powerful, particularly when they are heard by someone who cares and isn't judging you. Even more so, when that person is trained in *how* to listen. Many countries around the world offer breastfeeding helplines, where you can phone and be connected with a trained volunteer (often called a Breastfeeding Counsellor). The most well-known and international organisation to offer this service is La Leche League. The benefits of calling a helpline are that you will be connected with someone who has breastfed and who understands what you're going through (something you're not guaranteed to find with a standard therapist). This service is also free, or at least costs the same as a standard phone call. They tend to have extended opening hours, and there is no time limit to how long you speak to the volunteer for, making phonelines accessible for many people.

IBCLC Debrief

It's important to start this section by saying that there is no formal definition of a debrief for this sort of work. What many IBCLCs offer is a safe space to talk through your experience and understand it. We usually call this a debrief, but that's because it's short, snappy, and easy to understand. Many IBCLCs will offer this service over the phone or video call if an in-person meeting isn't possible for you. The principle is the same as talking to a volunteer over a helpline, but you'll have a predetermined amount of time, and the IBCLC will likely have a structure they follow to guide you through the debriefing process. They will also often tell you outright where you were let down or failed, whereas a breastfeeding counsellor will usually only listen with empathy. If you feel like you need answers, a debrief is a great step to take.

Therapy

As a trained therapist myself, it saddens me to have to start this section with a warning; not all therapists or counsellors are going to be able to support you with your feelings around breastfeeding. Often this seems to be simply down to a lack of experience with the issue, meaning they don't have the empathy and understanding they typically bring to their work. A couple of times a year, I even hear from clients that they booked in to see a therapist who simply told them that they were "too hung up" on breastfeeding or even that "fed is best."

Despite this, I am a huge advocate for therapy, and I think it should be universally accessible for everyone. A therapist can help you to unpick your feelings and figure out if they have a deeper root than your breastfeeding experience. It's important to screen any potential therapists when you're seeking support around breastfeeding grief and trauma, though. You can ask them when you initially reach out if they have experience with this, if they breastfed, and how they feel about the topic of grief around lactation. This should give you a good idea as to whether they'll be a good fit for you to work with,

Final Thoughts

Shortly after I started writing this book, my father died suddenly. In amongst the fog of early grief, I realised that what I was feeling was relevant to the work I was doing here. The only experience I had previously had that came close to the pain of losing my dad, was the pain of stopping breastfeeding before I wanted to. Of course, it wasn't precisely the same, but grieving for a loved one allowed me to see exactly why we call the loss, sadness, and anger that can come after lactation ends early "breastfeeding grief." It's real, and it can have a significant impact on your mood, self-esteem, and feelings as a mother.

While we've looked at a lot of reasons for breastfeeding failure in these pages that shine the spotlight on society, and while we obviously can't change how society looks after parents and mothers as they establish and maintain breastfeeding, we *can* begin to look at ways to offer support to help people through the grief and trauma that may come from being failed so badly. If we do this, maybe the next lactation experience will go more smoothly. Perhaps some will feel less guilty and ashamed, and better able to enjoy parenting with confidence and joy. Maybe there will be some anger stirred up that results in people demanding change in their local area. Maybe one person reading this will feel understood and just 1% better about their journey.

I hope that as you've read through this book, you have come to see that you have not failed, but you *have been failed*. This is no fault of your own, and if you're able to transfer some of that sadness, shame, or feelings of failure over to anger at the system that let you and your baby down, you may be able to channel that anger into something that feels powerful and healing for you, even if that something is to unapologetically enjoy parenting your little one without fear of how upset you'll feel if you see someone else breastfeeding.

References

Acquaye, S. N., & Spatz, D. L. (2021). An integrative review: The role of the doula in breastfeeding initiation and duration. *The Journal of Perinatal Education, 30*(1), 29-47. doi:10.1891/j-pe-d-20-00037

Adams, C. E., & Leary, M. R. (2007). Promoting self-compassionate attitudes toward eating among restrictive and Guilty Eaters. *Journal of Social and Clinical Psychology, 26*(10), 1120-1144. doi:10.1521/jscp.2007.26.10.1120

Ajmal, N., Khan, S. Z., & Shaikh, R. (2019). Polycystic ovary syndrome (PCOS) and genetic predisposition: A review article. *European Journal of Obstetrics & Gynecology and Reproductive Biology: X, 3,* 100060. doi:10.1016/j.eurox.2019.100060

Akhavan, A. A., Sandhu, S., Ndem, I., & Ogunleye, A. A. (2021). A review of gender affirmation surgery: What we know, and what we need to know. *Surgery, 170*(1), 336–340. doi:10.1016/j.surg.2021.02.013

Alcantara, J., Alcantara, J. D., & Alcantara, J. (2015). The chiropractic care of infants with breastfeeding difficulties. *EXPLORE, 11*(6), 468–474. doi:10.1016/j.explore.2015.08.005

Anttila-Hughes, J., Fernald, L. C., Gertler, P., Krause, P., & Wydick, B. (2018). Mortality from Nestlé's marketing of infant formula in low and middle-income countries. doi:10.3386/w24452

Araujo, M., Freitas, R., Lima, M., Kozmhinsky, V., Guerra, C., & Lima, G. et al. (2020). Evaluation of the lingual frenulum in newborns using two protocols and its association with breastfeeding. *Jornal De Pediatria, 96*(3), 379-385. https://doi.org/10.1016/j.jped.2018.12.013

Biggs, K. V., Fidler, K. J., Shenker, N. S., & Brown, H. (2020). Are the doctors of the future ready to support breastfeeding? A cross-sectional study in the UK. *International Breastfeeding Journal, 15*(1). doi:10.1186/s13006-020-00290-z

2022, J. (n.d.). Briefing: The cost of MPs in 2020-21. Retrieved April 1, 2023, from https://www.taxpayersalliance.com/briefing_the_cost_of_mps_in_2020_21

Britz, S. P., & Henry, L. (2011). PCOS and breastfeeding: What's the issue? *Journal of Obstetric, Gynecologic & Neonatal Nursing, 40.* doi:10.1111/j.1552-6909.2011.01244_10.x

Brown, A. (2016). What do women really want? lessons for breastfeeding promotion and education. Breastfeeding Medicine, 11(3), 102-110. doi:10.1089/bfm.2015.0175

Brown, A., Rance, J. & Bennett, P. (2016) Understanding the relationship between breastfeeding and postnatal depression: the role of pain and physical difficulties. *Journal of Advanced Nursing* 72(2), 273– 282. doi: 10.1111/jan.12832

Bryar, R. M., Cowley, D. S., Adams, C. M., Kendall, S., & Mathers, N. (2017). Health visiting in primary care in England: A crisis waiting to happen? *British Journal of General Practice, 67*(656), 102-103. doi:10.3399/bjgp17x689449

Chambers, A., Myers, S., Emmott, E. H., & Page, A. E. (2022). Emotional and informational social support from health visitors and breastfeeding outcomes in the UK. doi:10.31219/osf.io/37cke

Devereux, E. (2023, January 18). Survey shows half of health visitors in England intend to quit. Retrieved March 18, 2023, from https://www.nursingtimes.net/news/public-health/survey-shows-half-of-health-visitors-in-england-intend-to-quit-18-01-2023/#:~:text=As%20a%20result%20of%20the,or%20anxious%E2%80%9D%20(70%25).

Dijkstra, M. T., & Homan, A. C. (2016). Engaging in rather than disengaging from stress: Effective coping and perceived control. *Frontiers in Psychology, 7.* doi:10.3389/fpsyg.2016.01415

Edwards, C. N., & Miller, J. (2019). What is the evidence that chiropractic care helps sub-optimal breastfeeding? *Journal of Clinical Chiropractic Pediatrics, 18*(1).

Ekstrom, A., Widstrom, A., & Nissen, E. (2003). Breastfeeding support from partners and grandmothers: Perceptions of Swedish women. Birth, 30(4), 261-266. doi:10.1046/j.1523-536x.2003.00256.x

Emmott, E. H., & Mace, R. (2015). Practical support from fathers and grandmothers is associated with lower levels of breastfeeding in the UK millennium cohort study. *PLOS ONE, 10*(7). doi:10.1371/journal.pone.0133547

Flacking, R., Dykes, F., & Ewald, U. (2010). The influence of fathers' socioeconomic status and paternity leave on breastfeeding duration: A population-based Cohort Study. *Scandinavian Journal of Public Health, 38*(4), 337-343. doi:10.1177/1403494810362002

Baby Formula Crisis: Abbott enriched shareholders as factory needed repairs, records show. (2022, May 20). Retrieved April 1, 2023, from https://www.

theguardian.com/environment/2022/may/20/abbott-baby-formula-share-holder-profits

Boyd, J. E., Lanius, R. A., & McKinnon, M. C. (2018). Mindfulness-based treatments for posttraumatic stress disorder: A review of the treatment literature and neurobiological evidence. *Journal of Psychiatry & Neuroscience, 43*(1), 7–25. doi:10.1503/jpn.170021

Conversano, C., Orrù, G., Pozza, A., Miccoli, M., Ciacchini, R., Marchi, L., & Gemignani, A. (2021). Is mindfulness-based stress reduction effective for people with hypertension? A systematic review and meta-analysis of 30 years of evidence. *International Journal of Environmental Research and Public Health, 18*(6), 2882. doi:10.3390/ijerph18062882

García-Fragoso L, Jiménez D, Ortiz N, Quintero M. (2013). Father attitudes and knowledge about breastfeeding. *Boletin de la Asociacion Medica de Puerto Rico, 105*(4):37-40. PMID: 25154172.

Ghaheri, B.A., Cole, M., Fausel, S.C., Chuop, M., & Mace, J.C. (2017), Breastfeeding improvement following tongue-tie and lip-tie release: A prospective cohort study. *The Laryngoscope, 127*:1217-1223. https://doi.org/10.1002/lary.26306

Giannì, M. L., Lanzani, M., Consales, A., Bestetti, G., Colombo, L., Bettinelli, M. E., & Mosca, F. (2020). Exploring the emotional breastfeeding experience of first-time mothers: Implications for healthcare support. *Frontiers in Pediatrics, 8.* doi:10.3389/fped.2020.00199

Grandahl, M., Stern, J., & Funkquist, E. (2020). Longer shared parental leave is associated with longer duration of breastfeeding: A cross-sectional study among Swedish mothers and their partners. *BMC Pediatrics, 20*(1). doi:10.1186/s12887-020-02065-1

Grant, A. (2016). "I...don't want to see you flashing your bits around": Exhibitionism, othering and good motherhood in perceptions of public breastfeeding. *Geoforum, 71*, 52-61. doi:10.1016/j.geoforum.2016.03.004

Grassley, J., & Nelms, T. (2008). Understanding maternal breastfeeding confidence: A Gadamerian hermeneutic analysis of women's stories. *Health Care For Women International, 29*(8), 841-862. doi:10.1080/07399330802269527

Grisham, L. M., Rankin, L., Maurer, J. A., Gephart, S. M., & Bell, A. F. (2023). Scoping review of biological and behavioral effects of babywearing on mothers and infants. *Journal of Obstetric, Gynecologic & Neonatal Nursing, 52*(3), 191–201. doi:10.1016/j.jogn.2022.12.008

Gürol, A., & Polat, S. (2012). The effects of baby massage on attachment between mother and their infants. *Asian Nursing Research, 6*(1), 35-41. doi:10.1016/j. anr.2012.02.006

Haase, B., Brennan, E., & Wagner, C. L. (2019). Effectiveness of the IBCLC: Have we made an impact on the care of breastfeeding families over the past decade? *Journal of Human Lactation, 35*(3), 441-452. doi:10.1177/0890334419851805

Hansen, T. W. (2021). Narrative review of the epidemiology of neonatal jaundice. *Pediatric Medicine, 4*, 18–18. doi:10.21037/pm-21-4

Health Visitors Service Delivery Metrics. (n.d.). Retrieved March 18, 2023, from https://www.england.nhs.uk/statistics/statistical-work-areas/health-visitors/ health-visitors-service-delivery-metrics/

Huang, P., Yao, J., Liu, X., & Luo, B. (2019). Individualized intervention to improve rates of exclusive breastfeeding. *Medicine, 98*(47). doi:10.1097/md.000000 0000017822

ICD10 PTSD. (n.d.). Retrieved January 21, 2023, from https://estss.org/learn-about-trauma/icd10/

Kehinde, J., O'Donnell, C., & Grealish, A. (2023). The effectiveness of prenatal breastfeeding education on breastfeeding uptake postpartum: A systematic review. *Midwifery, 118*, 103579. doi:10.1016/j.midw.2022.103579

Kendall-Tackett, K. (2007). A new paradigm for depression in new mothers: The central role of inflammation and how breastfeeding and anti-inflammatory treatments protect maternal mental health. *International Breastfeeding Journal, 2*(1), 6. doi:10.1186/1746-4358-2-6

Kent, J. C., Mitoulas, L. R., Cregan, M. D., Ramsay, D. T., Doherty, D. A., & Hartmann, P. E. (2006). Volume and frequency of breastfeedings and fat content of breast milk throughout the day. *Pediatrics, 117*(3). doi:10.1542/peds.2005-1417

Khuzaiyah, S., Adnani, Q. E., Chabibah, N., Khanifah, M., & Lee, K. Y. (2022). A qualitative study on mothers' experiences attending an online infant massage class: "it is funny! I feel close to my baby!". *BMC Nursing, 21*(1). doi:10.1186/s12912-022-00952-9

Li, R., Fridinger, F., & Grummer-Strawn, L. (2002). Public perceptions on breastfeeding constraints. *Journal Of Human Lactation, 18*(3), 227-235. doi:10.1177/08934402018003004

Lisi, C., De Freitas, C., & Barros, H. (2021). The impact of formula industry marketing on breastfeeding rates in native and migrant mothers. *Breastfeeding Medicine, 16*(9), 725-733. doi:10.1089/bfm.2021.0041

Mahesh, P. K., Gunathunga, M. W., Arnold, S. M., Jayasinghe, C., Pathirana, S., Makarim, M. F., & Senanayake, S. J. (2018). Effectiveness of targeting fathers for breastfeeding promotion: Systematic review and meta-analysis. *BMC Public Health, 18*(1). doi:10.1186/s12889-018-6037-x

McDonald, H. M., Sherman, K. A., & Kasparian, N. A. (2022). How mindful awareness and psychological distress influence mother-infant bonding and maternal perceptions of infant temperament. *Mindfulness, 13*(4), 955–966. doi:10.1007/s12671-022-01848-0

Matthews, S. (2019). Self-stigma and addiction. *The Stigma of Addiction, 5-32.* doi:10.1007/978-3-030-02580-9_2

Milan, L., & Varescon, I. (2022). Self-stigma in alcohol use disorder: Involvement of guilt and shame in the progressive model. *Stigma and Health.* doi:10.1037/sah0000424

Mrljak, R., Arnsteg Danielsson, A., Hedov, G., & Garmy, P. (2022). Effects of infant massage: A systematic review. *International Journal of Environmental Research and Public Health, 19*(11), 6378. doi:10.3390/ijerph19116378

Navarro-Rosenblatt, D., & Garmendia, M. (2018). Maternity leave and its impact on breastfeeding: A review of the literature. *Breastfeeding Medicine, 13*(9), 589-597. doi:10.1089/bfm.2018.0132

Negin, J., Coffman, J., Vizintin, P. et al. (2016). The influence of grandmothers on breastfeeding rates: a systematic review. *BMC Pregnancy Childbirth 16,* 91https://doi.org/10.1186/s12884-016-0880-5

Newman, K. L., & Williamson, I. R. (2018). Why aren't you stopping now?!' exploring accounts of white women breastfeeding beyond six months in the east of England. *Appetite, 129,* 228-235. doi:10.1016/j.appet.2018.06.018

Obladen, M. (2009). Much ado about nothing: Two millennia of controversy on tongue-tie. *Neonatology, 97*(2), 83-89. https://doi.org/10.1159/000235682

Patel, S., & Patel, S. (2015). The effectiveness of lactation consultants and lactation counselors on breastfeeding outcomes. *Journal of Human Lactation, 32*(3), 530-541. doi:10.1177/0890334415618668

Phillips, R. (2013). The sacred hour: Uninterrupted skin-to-skin contact immediately after birth. *Newborn and Infant Nursing Reviews, 13*(2), 67-72. doi:10.1053/j.nainr.2013.04.001

Qiao, J., Dai, L., Zhang, Q., & Ouyang, Y. (2020). A meta-analysis of the association between breastfeeding and early childhood obesity. *Journal of Pediatric Nursing, 53*, 57-66. doi:10.1016/j.pedn.2020.04.024

Radbill S. (1981). Infant feeding through the ages. *Clinical Pediatrics, 20*(10):613–62.

Ramey-Collier, K., Jackson, M., Malloy, A., McMillan, C., Scraders-Pyatt, A., & Wheeler, S. (2023). Doula care: A review of outcomes and impact on birth experience. *Obstetrical & Gynecological Survey* 78(2):p 124-127 |DOI: 10.1097/OGX.0000000000001103

Ramoser, G., Guóth-Gumberger, M., Baumgartner-Sigl, S., Zoeggeler, T., Scholl-Bürgi, S., & Karall, D. (2019). Frenotomy for tongue-tie (frenulum linguae breve) showed improved symptoms in the short- and long-term follow-up. *Acta Paediatrica, 108*(10), 1861-1866. https://doi.org/10.1111/apa.14811

Shaw, S. C., & Devgan, A. (2018). Knowledge of breastfeeding practices in doctors and nurses: A questionnaire-based survey. *Medical Journal Armed Forces India, 74*(3), 217-219. doi:10.1016/j.mjafi.2016.11.015

Tschiderer, L., Seekircher, L., Kunutsor, S. K., Peters, S. A., O'Keeffe, L. M., & Willeit, P. (2022). Breastfeeding is associated with a reduced maternal cardiovascular risk: Systematic Review and meta-analysis involving data from 8 studies and 700 parous women. *Journal of the American Heart Association, 11*(2). doi:10.1161/jaha.121.022746

Federal appropriations for Breastfeeding. (n.d.). Retrieved April 1, 2023, from https://www.usbreastfeeding.org/federal-appropriations-for-breastfeeding.html

Verd, S., Ramakers, J., Vinuela, I., Martin-Delgado, M., Prohens, A., & Díez, R. (2021). Does breastfeeding protect children from covid-19? an observational study from pediatric services in Majorca, Spain. *International Breastfeeding Journal, 16*(1). doi:10.1186/s13006-021-00430-z

Noel-Weiss, J., Courant, G., & Woodend, A. K. (2008). Physiological weight loss in the breastfed neonate: a systematic review. *Open Medicine: A Peer-Reviewed, Independent, Open-Access Journal, 2*(4), e99–e110.

von Soest, T., Kvalem, I. L., Skolleborg, K. C., & Roald, H. E. (2011). Psychosocial changes after cosmetic surgery. *Plastic and Reconstructive Surgery, 128*(3), 765–772. doi:10.1097/prs.0b013e31822213f0

Wickes, I. G. (1953a). A history of infant feeding. Part I. Primitive peoples: Ancient works: Renaissance writers. *Archives of Disease in Childhood,* 28:151–158

Wickes, I.G. (1953b). A history of infant feeding. Part II. Seventeenth and eighteenth centuries. *Archives of Disease in Childhood, 28*:232–240.

Wickes, I. G. (1953d). A history of infant feeding. Part IV. Nineteenth century continued. *Archives of Disease in Childhood, 28*:416–422.

Take This Child and Suckle It for Me: Wet Nurses and Resistance in Ancient Israel. Biblical Theology Bulletin, 39 (4) (2009), pp. 180-189 <https://doi.org/10.1177/0146107909343550>